The High Frequency Game Changer

The High Frequency Game Changer

*How Automated Trading Strategies
Have Revolutionized the Markets*

**PAUL ZUBULAKE
SANG LEE**

Aite Group

WILEY

John Wiley & Sons, Inc.

Published by John Wiley & Sons, Inc., Hoboken, New Jersey.
Published simultaneously in Canada.

For general information on our other products and services or for technical support, please contact our Customer Care Department within the United States at (800) 762-2974, outside the United States at (317) 572-3993 or fax (317) 572-4002.

Wiley also publishes its books in a variety of electronic formats. Some content that appears in print may not be available in electronic books. For more information about Wiley products, visit our web site at www.wiley.com.

Library of Congress Cataloging-in-Publication Data

Zubulake, Paul.
    The high frequency game changer : how automated trading strategies have revolutionized the markets / Paul Zubulake, Sang Lee.
        p. cm. – (Wiley trading series)
    Includes index.
    ISBN 978-0-470-77038-2 (hardback); 978-1-118-01966-5 (ebk); 978-1-118-01967-2 (ebk); 978-1-118-01968-9 (ebk);
    1. Electronic trading of securities–United States.   2. Investment analysis–United States.
I. Lee, Sang.   II. Title.
    HG4515.95.Z83 2011
    332.64′20285–dc22

                                                                    2010045235

Printed in the United States of America

10 9 8 7 6 5 4 3 2 1

To my wife Karen and my sons, Zachary and Alexander, as well as my parents George and Mary and my sister Laura
—Paul Zubulake

To my wife Yong and my kids, Sage, Kayla, and Rhodes
—Sang Lee

Contents

Introduction

T he financial markets are part of everyone's life. People may not realize it but without a thriving capital market a country's economy would not exist. Open five days a week, fifty-two weeks a year, the daily ups and downs of the value of all markets causes consternation for the nation. The equity markets in particular are by far the most watched and dissected markets of all. They are covered by multiple financial television networks, hundreds of periodicals, not to mention thousands of internet sites. The equity markets' performance has become a daily ritual for society. There are of course many other markets that trade concurrently with the equity markets. Interest rates, currencies, commodities all have their own marketplaces listed and over-the-counter (OTC) that trade with large daily volumes.

So how does a marketplace work? This question may seem to be simple, but the answer is much more complex than the public realizes. In its simplest form a market matches up buyers and sellers at a certain price point. Once this occurs a transaction has taken place. These transactions take place on some type of execution venue. There are multiple types of venues where buyers and sellers are matched. In the equity markets, the markets have grown from a single entity, the New York Stock Exchange where all listed stocks are traded via a human based specialist model, to a vast network of electronic exchanges, ECNs (electronic communication networks), and dark pools. The transformation from a human based model to an electronic model has been one of the most important technological advances of modern investing. This transformation has not come without controversy. Without any doubt the most controversial aspect of this transformation has been the change in the way liquidity is provided to the many buyers and sellers in the market.

Liquidity is the amount of a security that is available on the bid/buy and offer/sell of a market, as well as the depth of both buyers and sellers. Conventional wisdom may see these market participants as the ones who already have a position in the security, but the reality is that the liquidity provider more commonly known as a market maker has no position at all. The growth of electronic trading was the ultimate game changer in the equity markets. Instead of calling in your orders to a broker who then would execute it via a floor exchange the order now is electronically transmitted to the various market venues.

The market had a new player, but it was not a person, it was a machine that could replicate the role of a liquidity provider but at a much higher speed and level of efficiency. It never gets tired and it can process information at a speed that a human could never do. Automated trading had been born and the markets have not looked back. The minds behind the machines have come from many different areas, the institutional trader, the floor trader, and the quantitative trader. Those who used their minds to trade have now developed many different types of trading strategies to provide the marketplace with orders to interact with the traditional players in the market. They trade often and in most cases hold their positions for very short time periods. High frequency trading is now part of the mainstream lore of the financial markets. Sometimes controversial and most times misunderstood, the role of the automated trader is one of major importance to today's ever-changing marketplace.

Acknowledgments

We would first like to thank Adam Honore, our research director at Aite Group. He was responsible for the technology content of this book and without Adam's contribution this book would have never have been completed. Additional thanks goes to the Aite Group team specifically the founding partners Gwenn Bezard, Frank Rizza, and Gerald Clemente. Special thanks to the Wiley team, Senior Editor Laura Walsh and Development Editor Judy Howarth. We appreciate their guidance and patience. Lastly we wanted to acknowledge the many contacts in the automated trading industry that we have spoken with over the last few years. Without their candid information, the knowledge and data produced through this book and our research would have never been possible.

CHAPTER 1

Birth of High Frequency Trading

Equity Markets Go Electronic

Electronic trading defines modern day trading in global equities markets. While one can point to many different factors for the eventual proliferation of electronic trading, it is important to acknowledge that without the basic market structure framework for accommodating electronic trading, today's market reality of sub-second trading and hyper-competitive market centers would be unthinkable.

As such, the electronification of the U.S. equity markets can be traced back to launch of Instinet in 1969, which predated the so-called Electronic Communication Networks (ECNs) by close to 30 years. Figure 1.1 shows the historical perspective.

Instinet provided a much needed service for buy-side firms looking for ways to trade listed securities in a private network. It became the largest alternative execution venue by the time the first generation alternative trading systems (ATSs) hit the U.S. equities market in the late 1990s.

Electronic trading occurred on the NASDAQ market first as market makers leveraged electronic communication tools to provide liquidity into the market. The 1987 crash, though, led to the development of SOES (Small Order Execution System), which provided automatic execution capabilities on a price-time priority. However, SOES only handled market or marketable limit orders and only executed up to 1,000 shares. In addition, SOES was only open for agency orders and prohibited any proprietary orders from market makers. While SOES is also often associated with the activities of SOES Bandits that took advantage of the new market reality,

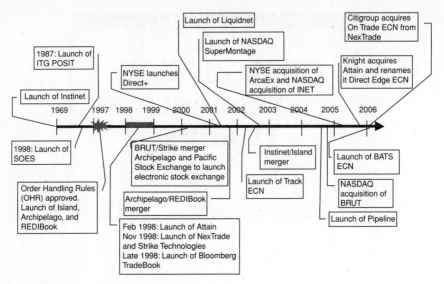

FIGURE 1.1   Historical Perspective on Market Competition in U.S. Equities Market
Source: Aite Group

it can certainly be viewed as one of the precursors to today's automated trading platforms that dominate the market.

Another set of regulatory change, the Order Handling Rules of 1997, triggered the birth of ECNs and the beginning of the end of the traditional floor-based exchange model characterized by open-outcry. After a decade of numerous regulatory changes, technology and business innovations, the electronification of the U.S. equities market had been completed. This set the foundation for the high frequency trading (HFT) firms.

DEFINING HIGH FREQUENCY TRADING

How can one cut through the misconception of high frequency trading? The subject has been defined in many ways with little satisfaction from the HFT community itself. The investing public has long viewed high frequency traders as market predators who game the market to their advantage. It is however, fair to say that during electronic trading infancy there was a good amount of predatory activity going on. This occurred as institutional investors who were just starting to self execute their own orders by using basic algorithms such as VWAP (volume weighted average price). This type of algorithm is one of many that slice up a large order into smaller orders that in theory will go undetected in the market place. Unfortunately for many institutional investors this theory did not hold up, as detecting a VWAP algorithm is a very simple process—"easy pickings" for any high frequency trader.

For most this would be enough evidence to prove that high frequency traders have not added any value to the markets. This is not the case at all, as the misunderstanding about how a market works has led to all the negative press about the subject. First, let's look at how a transaction is done. Every transaction needs a buyer and a seller to be matched off against each other. The price and size of the transaction need to be the same as well as the time of day. Using equities as an example, you have a buyer of 1000 shares of ABC stock at $10 and you need to have a seller of the same stock at the same price. Who would be a willing seller of ABC stock at $10? The first logical answer would be someone who already owns the stock. In a perfect world there would be someone willing to do such a transaction. But we do not live in a perfect world so in this case more often than not another party, who most likely has a position in the stock that does not exactly match what we are looking for, will need to provide an amount and price for one to transact against. Prior to electronic trading this role was held by a group of traders (market makers/specialists) who provided amount and prices (liquidity). Their role would be as a counterparty to the transaction. This is a relationship that is involved in every transaction in every market. Without a counterparty there would be no transactions of any type. This relationship is often misunderstood. Institutional and retail investors alike always want to be able to transact at any time at any price that is advantageous to them. In their minds the counterparty should be willing to provide liquidity without any change in price at all times of the day. Since we already have discussed that there is a lack of natural sellers (people/companies who already own the stock) the market maker/counterparty fills that need. This role of market maker is not a charitable one. Without an edge a market maker cannot make money and of course a business without profits is a business without participants.

Although we used the equity market as an example, the role of a market maker exists in all major markets. The interest rates (bond), currency, commodity, and option markets all need to have counterparties to complete a transaction. The more competition that exists in this role, the better the price provided will be.

As the financial markets migrated to an electronic marketplace, the role of the human-based market maker was disappearing. The only way to efficiently provide prices for buyers and sellers was to do so by electronic means. The market makers from the floor knew that the only way to do so properly was to have the most stable and fastest technology available. The life span of a slow market maker is too short to measure. Developing a system that had minimal latency was the key to success in the electronic world of market making. Speed is not the only variable to a successful operation, but without a low latency trading infrastructure you will not be able to compete.

Since speed is one of the components of high frequency trading, what are the other variables involved? As frequency is in the description it is logical to assume that the trading style leads to many transactions. This is of course is not a bad thing as an increase in volume leads to revenue increases in many areas of the business. Exchanges, brokers, technology providers, and telecom have all benefited from the increased participation in trading. The amount of volume attributed to HFT varies within each asset class, but it is safe to say without the volume generated from HFT firms the markets would look entirely different. Market making is the most common strategy for HFT, so if you make the assumption that every transaction has a market maker involved, the 50% volume threshold will be a good starting point in the equity markets.

The real issue remains how you silo the marketplace in a way that the press, politicians, regulators, and the public can understand. In today's equity market you can argue that everyone who buys and sells equities is using some sort of HFT type technology. Institutional customers either send their orders to their broker for execution or use an execution system to transact. Retail customers now execute their orders via an online broker. Orders are sent and filled immediately and prices are reported back in seconds.

What then separates the high frequency trading community from the rest of the investing world? It comes down to two subjects: trading strategy and holding time.

There are multiple trading strategies employed by the HFT community. The two main areas are liquidity provision and arbitrage. Both of these strategies require a low latency trading infrastructure with reliance on receiving live market data as trades occur. In a perfect world a market-making strategy would buy the bid and sell the offer all day every day. They would make the small spread and everyone would go home happy. Of course this is the not the case and a market maker will always adjust their prices and size available based on the prevailing price action in the market. It really is all related to supply and demand. As the old trading saying goes, more buyers than sellers will drive the market higher and the opposite is true as well. This may seem simplistic, but this is how the price discovery process works. There always has been and always will be an advantage to those who provide liquidity: If they were not there, there would be no market. So despite the criticism the new market makers of the electronic trading world will continue to make technology investments and fine tune their algorithms to stay ahead of their competition. New entrants are always welcome and as long as they are willing to make the appropriate investment, the playing field is truly level. The investing public has been rewarded with narrowing spreads and lower commission costs. This is a fact that gets thrown out the window when markets are trading lower and the public is losing money, so today's market makers live in a fickle world and understand that this is the price of doing business.

Riskless arbitrage is the action of buying and selling the same security on two different venues at the same time. Although the opportunities in this area have decreased significantly due to increased competition there is still money being made. The equity market remains the market of choice for arbitrageurs. All is not guaranteed in this strategy as there is always a risk of missing out on one part of the trade and being left with a money-losing position.

Statistical arbitrage (stat/arb) is another HFT strategy that is difficult to be executed without a low latency trading infrastructure. An example of an opportunity for stat/arb traders comes from outside investors who are either accumulating or liquidating a position of stock that is a member of an index. Once that price of the individual stock changes, the correlated index price also has to change. Other derivatives such as options or futures of the index also have to update. These opportunities are short lived and competed for by various traders. The competition for such trades is an essential component of how high frequency traders contribute to market efficiencies.

Since the majority of the listed markets are electronic and investors of all types are using technology that can be defined as high frequency, the holding time of each trade or investment is the ultimate differentiator between the professional high frequency trader and others. There is no absolute time that a HFT holds a position, but as a general rule the time is measured in seconds. It could be in milliseconds or microseconds or in the near future nanoseconds, but the reality is the holding time is for very small periods of time. Can a HFT hold position for a longer time period? The answer is yes and there will always be circumstances when holding times vary. However, as long as the market venues continue to improve their technology and the regulators do not require orders to be held for a certain time period, the race to zero will continue. A change to sub-penny pricing in the equity world would be the major catalyst for holding times to be reduced even further.

WHO ARE THE HIGH FREQUENCY TRADERS?

For most Wall Street firms out there, 2008 was a year to forget and move beyond as quickly as possible. For a small group of firms based mostly outside downtown Manhattan in Chicago, Dallas, and Kansas City, however, 2008 was a banner year with record performance.

So-called "high frequency prop shops" thrived during a year characterized by massive economic downturn, job losses, record volume, and volatility, while traditional asset managers, large hedge funds, and all of the bulge bracket firms suffered.

Until recently, high frequency prop shops have been flying under the radar, preferring to take a back seat as bulge bracket firms and high-flying hedge funds soaked up all the glory and publicity. While the Goldmans and Morgans of the world were building up their global empire, firms with names like GETCO and Tradebot were fine-tuning their trading models and low-latency technology infrastructure. Today, the growing market clout of these high frequency trading firms can no longer be ignored. As a collective group, they represent a significant force in trading and market structure, and will play a more public role in the global securities markets for many more years to come, whether they like it or not.

There are many proprietary trading firms, including those that reside within large broker/dealers, which until 2008 were major sources of revenue for the bulge bracket firms like Goldman Sachs, Morgan Stanley, Credit Suisse, and more. Based on the Aite Group's interviews with leading independent proprietary trading firms (i.e., not affiliated with a bulge bracket firm), an elite group of firms numbering no more than 15 currently account for a significant percentage of overall average daily trade volume in U.S. equities. Over the last couple of years, their presence has been clearly felt well beyond equities and into other exchange-traded, liquid markets such as U.S. equity options and global futures as well as highly liquid OTC (over-the-counter) markets, such as FX (foreign exchange). These firms have also moved beyond U.S. borders, especially into the European equities market.

The high frequency, high-volume trading game is being played by many different types of players. In today's competitive trading market, the high frequency trading community consists of market makers that rely on automated trading technology, low-latency agency brokers, statistical arbitrage hedge funds, and high frequency proprietary trading firms:

- *Regulated market makers.* Leading wholesalers such as Citadel, Knight, and ATD have carved out a nice market for the automated market making business. They are regulated market makers that have employed technology to enhance the overall operations of a traditional market making role.
- *Statistical arbitrage hedge funds.* Statistical arbitrage hedge funds have also added to the overall trading volume in recent years, using high-powered computer models to identify and execute tiny arbitrage opportunities across hundreds if not thousands of names in milliseconds.
- *Low-latency brokers.* Less well-known, but highly technology-driven, low-latency agency brokers such as Lime Brokerage drive an incredible amount of volume on behalf of their stat/arb and prop trading clients.
- *Clearing.* On the clearing side, firms such as Wedbush, Penson, Fortis, and Assent have carved out a nice business catering to the high frequency trading community through aggressive pricing and their ability to handle large volumes.

The burgeoning independent proprietary trading firms scattered across the United States have been leading the charge. These active trading firms have emerged to level the playing field and replace traditional market makers and specialist firms, becoming an indispensable source of liquidity for the U.S. equities market. While small in number (estimated to be 10 to 15 firms at most, with significant trading operations), these firms have energized the overall trading market, pushing for greater technology innovation, testing the limits of speed and, most importantly, providing liquidity to the various execution venues. A set of common high frequency proprietary trading firms' characteristics includes the following:

- *Technology vendor first, trading second.* Most of these firms behave and function like a technology firm. Leading proprietary trading firms are filled with Ph.D.s, typically in areas such as mathematics, physics, computer science, and statistics. Every problem these firms face, they look for solutions based on technology, which enables them to keep a streamlined operation with limited number of people. First-tier proprietary trading firms (top 10 to 15 firms) have built their IT infrastructure from scratch, rarely relying on third-party vendors.

- *More than just speed.* Systematic black box trading requires a lot of speed, and certain high frequency firms are obsessive about maintaining a trading infrastructure that can handle the peaks and valleys of a trading day with minimum levels of latency. In addition to speed, proprietary trading firms believe that the trading infrastructure must be resilient, reliable, and predictable.

- *Trading models as a competitive differentiator.* In the end, these firms' bread and butter are their trading models. Development of new and constant enhancements of existing trading models enables high frequency trading firms to stay a step ahead of the competition. Leveraging their Ph.D.s' brainpower and cutting-edge trading technology platforms, proprietary trading firms have created systematic trading models that drive significant volume into the marketplace.

- *Keeping a low profile.* Historically, since all of these firms are trading with their own money, generating publicity is one of the lowest priorities for a prop shop. However, with today's challenging economic conditions and the threat of wholesale regulatory changes that might threaten their business model, these traditionally publicity-shy proprietary trading firms will have to open up to validate their market importance.

Growth of these prop trading firms has contributed greatly to today's market reality of exploding trade volume, tight spreads, decreased average trade size, and focus on speed and technology. Over the years, traditional market makers have been replaced by regulated market makers that have fully embraced technology (i.e., Citadel, Knight, ATD, etc.). High frequency proprietary trading firms have also stepped into the void, providing much-needed liquidity and tighter spreads while at the same time leveling the playing field, making it possible for anyone with good technology and sophisticated trading models to become an impact player. With the evolution of market structure, driven by rapid adoption of electronic trading and democratization of access to market data, these de facto low latency market making firms have emerged to become a major force in the U.S. equities market.

IMPACT OF HIGH FREQUENCY TRADING

The ultimate impact of high frequency proprietary trading firms can be felt in many different areas of the institutional trading market. What appears to be a never-ending pursuit of low-latency is certainly one of the more well documented byproducts of firms engaging in high frequency trading activities. The top 10 to 15 proprietary trading firms are typically self-sufficient when it comes to IT development. Despite this, an entire ecosystem of third-party technology providers has emerged during the last few years to accommodate the growth of the needs of other high frequency trading firms, including hedge funds, brokers, and second-tier prop shops ranging from high-performance feed handlers and middleware messaging bus to strategy generation platforms and outsourced low-latency market data services. Execution venues have courted order flow aggressively from the high frequency trading community through allure of ownership, a race to the bottom with transaction costs, and upgrades in technology. Highlights of the high frequency trading community's overall impact on the institutional trading market include the following:

- *Chasing the speed of light.* The focus on low latency is built into the DNA of each high frequency trading firm. For this community, every microsecond counts, and the push for faster execution turnaround is a never-ending endeavor. In essence, the high frequency trading firms generate profit by having the right combination of IT infrastructure to receive market data first and acting on changing market conditions faster than other firms to both cancel out and execute orders. Not surprisingly, the growing market clout of high frequency prop shops has also pushed broker/dealers and various exchanges and ATSs to upgrade their own trading infrastructure to keep up with the demand. Industry pursuit of low latency has also created a burgeoning third-party technology market:
- *Technology is king.* In today's new world order, driven by speed and microsecond executions, a clear competitive differentiator is technology. High frequency trading firms typically rely on internal builds to develop their own IT infrastructure and minimize latency. In order to compete against and accommodate the growing needs of high frequency trading firms, the rest of the capital markets have committed billions of dollars annually to technology growth.

- *Tighter spreads and lower transaction costs.* There are many reasons why spreads have tightened and transaction costs keep going down. One of the most significant reasons behind the tightening of spreads was the introduction of decimalization in 2001. Wide adoption of electronic trading and algorithmic trading overall has also contributed to tightening spreads and a decrease in transaction costs. High frequency proprietary trading firms have led the industry in recent years in terms of adoption of electronic trading, employing automated market making strategies to maintain tight spreads, and also forcing most execution venues to maintain sub-penny transaction fee schedules.

- *Major source of liquidity and trading volume.* Active participation of high frequency trading firms has typically resulted in rapid growth in trading volume and overall liquidity as can be seen on popular ECNs, such as BATS and Direct Edge. Another interesting number to examine is the dramatic increase in overall trading volume of the NYSE-listed marketplace. In 2006, as Regulation National Market System (Reg NMS) was being implemented, the NYSE launched its hybrid market and averaged approximately 3 billion shares in daily trade volume. Two years later, with conditions more conducive to participation from high frequency trading firms, the NYSE average close to 6.5 billion shares at the end of 2008.

- *Expansion of the maker-taker model.* Island, one of the clear innovators in the ECN industry, was the first execution venue to introduce the maker-taker model, which has become the de facto pricing model of today's U.S. equities market. By offering a rebate for providing liquidity and charging for taking liquidity, Island created an ideal transaction model to attract aggressive participation of high frequency trading firms. Now, the maker-taker model has migrated over to the U.S. equities options market and European cash equities market, illustrating the expanding influence of the high frequency trading firms beyond U.S. equities. While some firms do rely on rebates for liquidity provision to make money, most proprietary trading firms interviewed for this report indicated that the rebate is a bonus. If rebates did not exist, their models would simply adjust to look for additional profits elsewhere.

- *Active investor in market structure.* In addition to trading, certain firms within the high frequency trading community have also become active investors in various execution venues. Most venues that have succeeded in attracting investments from the high frequency trading firms have done quite well, gradually mounting a serious challenge to existing exchanges which, in turn, will no doubt generate a nice return on investment for that high frequency trading ownership.

- *Moving beyond equities.* The growing presence of high frequency proprietary trading firms goes well beyond just cash equities. Looking to diversify and seek new market opportunities, these firms have opted to move into other asset classes, leveraging their technology and trading models. Their presence is felt across all exchange-traded products, including U.S. equity options and global futures, and even in OTC products such as FX. In all these products, general market characteristics in recent years have been tightening spreads and explosive trading volume. All of the products have underlying market infrastructure capable of supporting electronic trading as well as clearly defined centralized clearing infrastructure. In the case of FX, the combination of robust prime brokerage model has enabled high frequency trading firms to actively participate in the market.

Much has been written about the current market predicament. The subprime blow-up, excesses of the investment banking industry, and evidence of massive financial fraud have shaken the fundamental stability of global financial markets. At the height of the 2008 market roller coaster, shortsellers were blamed for the collapse of financial stocks, and the overall public perception of the hedge fund community hit a historic low. In addition, Bernie Madoff's massive Ponzi scheme has worsened the overall market perception of alternative investment vehicles altogether. With the Obama administration now in place, new regulations in the securities industry appear almost inevitable. Much attention will no doubt be focused on the hedge fund market. Tougher regulations are certainly needed to ensure trust in global markets is restored.

One danger is that some of these regulations will be too sweeping, generalizing every firm in nontraditional asset management or broker/dealer area as a potential threat to the future stability of the global financial services industry. One could argue that Madoff's industry reputation enabled the Ponzi scheme to last so long right under the nose of the regulators. Unfortunately, the current public outcry over the Madoff affair could trigger an extreme regulatory response without regulators fully understanding the fundamental changes the market has undergone over the last decade.

High frequency traders, small in number and low in public profile, simply cannot be lumped into the general category of harmless little alternative investment vehicles or brokers/dealers that need to be tightly

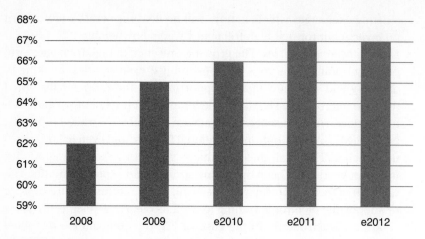

FIGURE 1.2 Adoption of High Frequency Trading
Source: Aite Group

regulated. The reality is that the high frequency trading community (i.e., regulated electronic market makers, stat/arb hedge funds, and high frequency prop shops) now combines to form more than 60% of the average daily volume in U.S. equities. As a result, any regulatory action designed to curtail their trading activity must take into account potential consequences of this liquidity evaporating. Any potential regulation designed to restore faith in the global financial markets must include active participation of the high frequency trading community so they can become part of the solution. Figure 1.2 estimates the growing adoption of high frequency trading.

In the end, one must not look at today's market reality, heavily dominated by high frequency trading firms, as either good or bad. Instead, it must be examined from an evolutionary perspective. Not too long ago, human market makers and specialists dominated the U.S. equities market, benefiting greatly from access to information that the rest of the market did not have. However, the advent of electronic trading, various regulatory changes (Order Handling Rules [OHR] of 1997, Regulation ATS, and Reg NMS), the emergence of ECNs, increased market fragmentation, and availability of low-latency trading technology have opened up the next stage of market evolution. In this stage, technology-savvy trading firms take over the essential role of liquidity providers to ensure high levels of liquidity, tight spreads, and market stability.

Today's dominance of high frequency proprietary trading firms is just a byproduct of all of the changes that the market has experienced over the last decade, and there is nothing cynical about the actual role that these firms currently provide. They simply provide the much-needed service of offering liquidity into various markets and generating profits on tiny spreads. In other words, these firms are the new market makers of the present and future unless other competitive forces come into play to alter the current market arrangement.

BUILDING A HIGH FREQUENCY TRADING TEAM

Building a high frequency trading team is obviously not an easy endeavor. The team needs to understand trading and market structure as well as should have overall expertise in multiple areas of technology. The original high frequency traders were already trading in some capacity prior to starting their own operations. Outside of the obvious need for funding, their other immediate need would be to have a chief technology officer who understands all the needs of a trading shop. A trading shop needs to have connectivity to the trading venues and to the back offices of the exchanges and the necessary broker/dealer relationships. Dealing with exchanges, brokers, and telecom companies is never easy and the necessary relationships have to be made.

When it comes to the recruitment process, each firm will look at candidates in different ways. Some will only recruit the top quantitative minds from the top universities that are available. Others prefer trading experience, with or without any technology background. Some want a competitive attitude with winning being the only thing that matters. Striking a balance is the key to many successful firms as only one firm can be the fastest. Having to compete with the established large HFT shops that have large budgets is a task not worth spending your time and money on. The goal should be to be the smartest as opposed to the fastest. The trading strategy that you employ will be the differentiating aspect of your firm. A sound trading strategy is the way to begin. This is not a guarantee for success, but there is no other way for a new entrant to start.

Choosing your asset class is one step that is very important. To think that you will be able to trade on multiple markets that have different market structures is a pipedream. If you have a background in foreign exchange or futures trading the best bet is to start with what your familiar with. The equity markets have been the starting ground for most traders, but the space is very crowded and you may find out that your strategy is always behind. Trading globally has received much hype, but most international markets have more barriers to entry than your typical U.S. market. New entrants who enter the market must understand how competitive the business is and what type of sacrifice is necessary. Working for an existing firm at any level is a great starting point. Always remember to check your ego at the door and learn as much as possible. Once you feel confident in your strategy and have learned all the ins and outs of running a trading operation, you can go out on your own and see if you make the grade.

CHAPTER 2

Market Structure

U pheaval and uncertainty are two words that can be used to describe the current status of the U.S. equities market. The hostile institutional trading environment continues as shrinking commission rates and spreads have driven many experienced equities traders out of business altogether. Electronic trading has established itself as the main mode of trading, but uncertainties abound that are driven by regulations and the evolution of sophisticated trading strategies and technologies.

The adoption of Regulation National Market System (Reg NMS) in 2005 institutionalized the legitimacy of electronic trading and has forced all of the major exchanges to launch trading platforms with automated execution capability to remain competitive in the post-Reg NMS market structure. Reg NMS has also ushered in a wave of market consolidation as NASDAQ and the New York Stock Exchange (NYSE) sought to solidify their competitive positions: NASDAQ acquired INET, a leading electronic communication network (ECN), and the NYSE linked up with ArcaEx, a leading all-electronic regional exchange (and a former ECN) to create what appeared to be a de facto duopoly in the U.S. equities market.

However, this trend of consolidation was short-lived. Soon after the announcements of the NYSE and NASDAQ combinations, numerous ATSs (alternative trading systems) and ECNs emerged, sensing new market opportunities in the post-Reg NMS environment. As a result, market fragmentation has occurred once again, similar to the market fragmentation that was prevalent in the NASDAQ market immediately following the adoption of the Order Handling Rules (OHR) of 1997.

Traders in today's U.S. equities market have a plethora of options when it comes to trade execution. They can certainly send orders to major market centers such as the NYSE and NASDAQ, but they can also rely on numerous regional exchanges as well as various ECNs and ATSs in the marketplace. A growing number of buy-side firms are getting their trades done in private trading networks, such as Liquidnet and Pipeline. Not to be outdone, most major brokers have also developed internal crossing engines to provide yet another venue for trade execution.

As a result, the current status of the U.S. equities market is marked by competition, fragmentation, and the potential for consolidation. Smaller, privately owned or broker-driven execution venues are emerging to take advantage of potential market opportunities in the post-Reg NMS market structure, which is leading to more competition and fragmentation. At the same time, however, the two largest pools of liquidity, the NYSE and NASDAQ, have set their eyes across the pond and are looking to combine their operations with Euronext and the London Stock Exchange (LSE), respectively.

This chapter traces the evolution of the U.S. equities market, starting from the adoption of the OHR in 1997.

ORDER HANDLING RULES OF 1997

Our analysis begins with the SEC (securities and exchange commission) regulatory decisions of 1997 to rein in widespread corruption and illegal order handling by NASDAQ market makers. The OHR of 1997 sought to create a more orderly market in which all market participants would have access to greater market transparency and improved execution rates. The OHR consist of two rules:

- *Limit Order Handling Rule.* This rule mandates that market makers receiving limit orders inside their spread must handle these orders in one of three ways. The first two options effectively result in market makers narrowing their spread or reducing their profits:
  - Incorporate the price into their quote in NASDAQ's quote montage.
  - Execute the limit order immediately.
  - Send the limit order to another market participant (other market makers or ECNs) that will display the order.

- *Quote Display Rule.* This rule bans market makers from posting one quote in the NASDAQ quote montage and a different quote for the same stock in an alternative trading network. However, under the same rule, dual quoting is permissible if the alternative trading network has a direct link to NASDAQ and has the capability to post its best bid and offer on the NASDAQ quote montage.

Combined, the two tenets of the OHR ensured that ECNs would thrive in the NASDAQ market. ECNs became the main outlet for unwanted limit orders from market makers. Large buy-side firms became attracted to ECNs because of their ability to execute orders anonymously and to minimize market impact. For all market participants, the rapid, automatic matching capability of the ECNs substantially lowered transaction fees, which directly translated into substantial cost savings.

GROWTH OF ELECTRONIC COMMUNICATION NETWORKS

One of the most important events of the last decade in the U.S. equities market has been the introduction and evolution of ECNs. Prior to the OHR of 1997, the only ECN-like platform with notable liquidity was Instinet. Instinet began its operations in 1969, nearly three decades before the creation of the first NASDAQ ECNs.

As a category, ECNs are a fully electronic subset of ATSs that automatically and anonymously match orders based on price-time priority. ECNs function as an execution venue similar to exchanges, but from a regulatory perspective, they are broker-dealers. Unlike other agency broker-dealers, ECNs are allowed to post their best bid and offer on NASDAQ's quote montage. In this way, ECNs are able to participate in NASDAQ and compete head-to-head against other market participants for order flow. The term "ECN" only applies to those private networks that have been recognized as such under the SEC's ECN Display Alternative Rule. Over the last nine years, ECNs have gone through a phase of rapid growth followed by consolidation.

At the height of their existence, ECNs exhibited two very distinct business models. Figure 2.1 breaks down the original models. These models are:

- *Best execution-centric.* The remaining ECNs followed the best execution-centric model dictated by the reality of a lack of internal

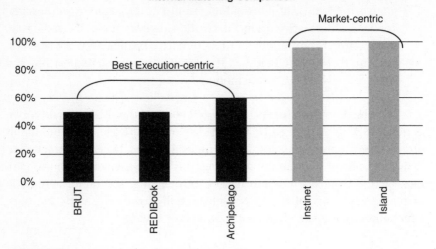

FIGURE 2.1   Two Business Models of ECNs
Source: ECNs
Market-centric. Initially, only Instinet and Island truly represented this model. Under this model, most orders that entered their trading systems were matched internally and were rarely routed out of their platform to other execution venues. In general, those utilizing Instinet and Island were more concerned about speed of execution than with execution price

liquidity. These ECNs (e.g., Archipelago, REDIBook, BRUT, etc.) would look to match orders internally first and then, using smart order routing technologies, would route the unmatched orders to various execution venues with the best price. Not surprisingly, the best price often took precedence over speed of execution under this model.

In the first quarter (Q1) of 2002, only Instinet and Island could claim to be true execution venues with high levels of internal liquidity. Other ECNs used a hybrid model of order execution and order routing; some focused more on order routing than others—again driven by the reality of a lack of internal liquidity. Figure 2.2 shows the Average Daily Trade (ADT) of the ECN's in 2002.

In the end, a true value proposition of an ECN was its ability to match orders internally, based on a high level of liquidity. Although order routing was a value-added service, it increasingly become marginalized as the popularity of direct market access providers (i.e., aggregators), such as Lava Trading, continued to increase.

In terms of direct ECN-to-ECN competition, the initial spotlight was on Island and Instinet. Over the years of competition, Instinet continued to

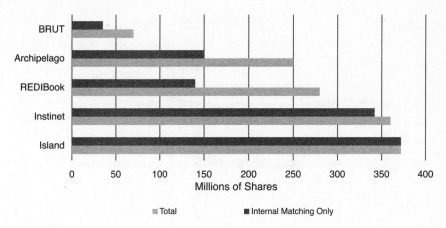

FIGURE 2.2 Average Daily Trade Volume of ECNs in 2002
Source: ECNs, Aite Group

rely on order flow from its traditional client base of institutional traders and market makers. Island, on the other hand, focused on the under-served but rapidly growing client segments of hedge funds, proprietary trading desks, program trading desks, and retail flow. Instinet also did not succumb to the commission compression that was impacting all of the other ECNs until it started losing market share to Island in 2001. Finally, by the end of 2001, Island became the largest ECN in NASDAQ. In order to remain competitive, Instinet did the only thing it could do in June of 2002: acquire Island for more than US$500 million in cash. Figure 2.3 shows how the landscape changed in 2001.

Overall, ECNs made tremendous progress in penetrating NASDAQ over the last nine years and accounted for approximately 57% of the market share within NASDAQ by the end of 2005. Figure 2.4 displays how the ECNs penetrated NASDAQ.

NASDAQ's answer to the ECN threat was the launch of SuperMontage, its automated trading platform, in late 2002. However, SuperMontage's competitiveness fell quite short of NASDAQ's expectations and instead led to an actual decline of market share. In Q3 2002, prior to the launch of SuperMontage, NASDAQ accounted for approximately 24% of the market share. By the end of Q2 2004, that figure had declined to 15%. Figure 2.5 shows the declining market share of SuperMontage.

NASDAQ was at a crossroads, and something drastic had to be done to retain its leadership position in the U.S. equities execution market. In the end, NASDAQ resorted to an aggressive acquisition program.

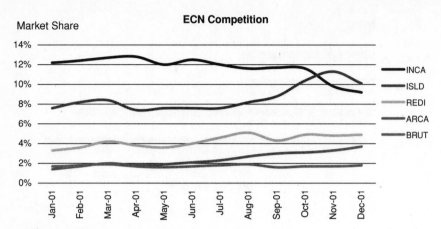

FIGURE 2.3 Changing Competitive Landscape
Source: NASDAQ

On the other hand, penetration of the listed market by ECNs had been disappointing at best. The most notable exception had been the trading of exchanged traded funds (ETFs), which originally started in the American Stock Exchange (AMEX). Overall, however, ECNs' foray into the listed market had failed to produce any significant gains. Examining the NYSE market alone, ECNs accounted for approximately 5% of the NYSE trade share volume at the end of 2004. However, by the end of 2005, much

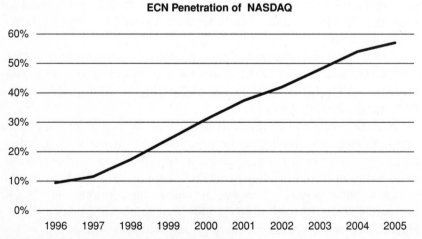

FIGURE 2.4 Market Share of ECNs in NASDAQ
Source: NASDAQ, ECNs, Aite Group

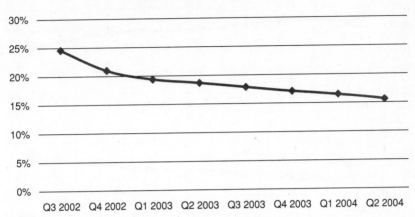

FIGURE 2.5 Unsuccessful Launch of SuperMontage
Source: NASDAQ, Aite Group

progress had been made by the combination of INET, BRUT (with its free DOT program), Bloomberg TradeBook, and ArcaEx to gain a foothold into the NYSE. The fact that the competition had been opened up as a result of impending Reg NMS in the electronic trading market also played a key role in making some of the ECNs viable alternatives to trading NYSE stocks. By the end of 2005, the ECN market share of the NYSE reached 7%. Figure 2.6 shows the ECN penetration of NYSE listed stocks.

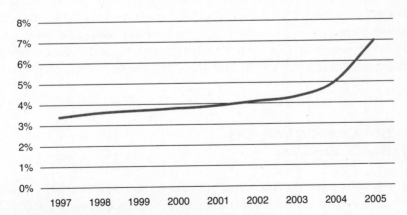

FIGURE 2.6 ECN Penetration of NYSE-Listed Stocks
Source: NYSE Euronext, ECNs, Aite Group

FIGURE 2.7 Declining Market Share of NYSE
Source: NYSE, ECNs, Aite Group
Note: Market share figures for NASDAQ and PCX include trade prints from internal matching at broker/dealers and other execution venues

Overall, the NYSE had been experiencing losses in market share in NYSE-listed trading since 2000 when its market share stood at well above 80%. By January of 2006, that market share had plummeted to 71.7%. Competitive pressures continued to increase, not only from ECNs, but also from ATSs that specialize in block trading as well as other exchanges (most notably NASDAQ). Regulatory pressure from Reg NMS and customer demand also mounted and forced the NYSE to initiate a Hybrid Market strategy. At the same time, the NYSE looked to take a bold step toward the electronic market by quietly seeking out a potential partner. Figure 2.7 shows the declining market of the NYSE market share and the rise of its competitors.

REGULATION NATIONAL MARKET SYSTEM

In early 2004 when the SEC came out with its proposed Reg NMS, which was designed to create a more integrated market system, most of the debate had centered around Reg NMS's controversial views on trade throughs, with some industry insiders accusing the SEC of introducing a central limit order book (CLOB) disguised in sheep's clothing. After a year of much heated discussion, the waiting game ended with the expected three–two vote by the Commission in passing the regulation.

The SEC's main argument for Reg NMS can be summed up by the following considerations:

- *Protection of individual investors.* One unifying theme of the SEC has been its focus on protecting the interests of individual investors. This type of thinking goes to the heart of the most controversial area of Reg NMS, which is the Trade-Through Rule. This rule, in essence, takes a very narrow view of what best possible execution should be by focusing on best price. While this may be beneficial for the individual investors in general, some of the largest institutional investors would probably argue otherwise.
- *Recognition of available technology and the need to change the Intermarket Trading System (ITS).* The viability of the ITS, which began operations in 1979, has been the subject of debate for over a decade. Finally, however, the SEC decided that given the availability of cost-effective connectivity solutions provided by third-party technology providers, it is no longer necessary to operate an artificial national market system based on outdated IT infrastructure.
- *Leveling the playing field in terms of regulation.* With the existence of multitudes of execution venues, the SEC has opted to create an overarching national regulation which will dictate the way the entire national market system will behave instead of singling out specific stock exchanges.

In the end, the SEC wanted a set of rules which can be applied uniformly across all U.S. equities market centers to improve market transparency and to guarantee fair access for individual investors. The core of Reg NMS is composed of four key rules:

- *Trade-Through Rule (Rule 611).* The basic idea of the Trade-Through Rule (also known as the Order Protection Rule) is to protect limit orders of investors by forbidding a particular market center from trading through another market with a better price and executing the order at an inferior price. The Trade-Through Rule within the ITS plan has existed for many years, although only within the exchange-listed stocks with little enforcement. Under the new Trade-Through Rule, order protection will extend to NASDAQ stocks as well as block trading and small orders (i.e., so-called "100 share order"). In addition, faced with the reality of floor and electronic markets, the Trade-Through Rule would protect only automated quotes. There are built-in exceptions to the Trade-Through Rule, including intermarket sweep (enabling firms to simultaneously sweep multiple market centers at different price levels) and flickering quotes. The Rule would also require all market centers to develop and enforce policies and procedures to deter trade throughs. Perhaps the most controversial part of the Trade-Through Rule was the two alternative versions the SEC proposed:

- *Top-of-book (TOB)*. This first alternative (i.e., "Market BBO Alternative") would only protect the Best Bids and Offers (BBOs) leaving the market requirement quite similar to the one which currently exists under the ITS plan.
- *Depth-of-book (DOB)*. This second alternative (i.e., "Voluntary Depth Alternative") would protect the entire depth-of-book beyond the BBOs, but only required market centers to display DOB on a voluntary basis. This is the virtual CLOB alternative that caught most market participants off guard when it was introduced.

- *Access Rule (Rule 610)*. This rule tackles a number of issues surrounding access to NMS stock quotes. First, the Access Rule addresses the hotly debated ECN access fees by mandating that any market center can charge an access fee capped at US\$0.003 per share. Second, the rule encourages ITS/UTP members to use private links to connect to other members, thereby implicitly signaling the eventual phase-out of ITS. Third, the rule requires market centers to develop and establish procedures to prevent locked or cross markets. Finally, the rule lowers the threshold of fair access as stipulated in Regulation ATS from the current 20% to 5% of the average daily volume of a given stock.
- *Market Data Rules and Plans (Rules 601 and 603)*. This rule addresses market data availability issues and the need to link market data revenue and usefulness of data. First, the rule would enable market centers and their members to independently distribute market data with or without fees while still mandating market centers to report their best quotes and trades to their designated Securities Information Processors (SIPs). Second, a new formula will be used to allocate market data revenue, taking into account the value of quotes and trades into the consolidated data stream. Finally, the rule proposes a new definition of "consolidated display" to include only data on NBBO (national best bid and offer) and consolidated last sale information.

- *Sub-Penny Rule (Rule 612).* Considered to be the least controversial aspect of Reg NMS, this rule would prohibit market participants from displaying and accepting quotes of NMS stocks in sub-penny increments with an exception for those stocks priced below US$1.00 per share.

Combined, these four rules make up Reg NMS, which the SEC hopes will create a true national market system in which key rules will be applied uniformly across market centers and ultimately protects the rights of individual investors.

On April 6, 2005, the SEC made its final decision on the proposed Reg NMS. As expected by most, the final vote was three to two, with the Chairman siding with the two Democratic Commissioners. As a result, the following deadlines for implementation have been issued (as shown in Figure 2.8).

The SEC substantially delayed the implementation of Reg NMS by taking a more cautious, phased-in approach which was not completed until October 2007, over one year past its originally scheduled completion date. However, most of the execution venues worked feverishly to become fully Reg NMS-compliant, regardless of the implementation delay.

- As is typical with most SEC regulations—which tend to be influenced by industry and political pressures—it is tough to single out an

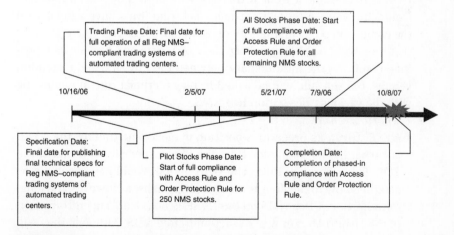

FIGURE 2.8 Timeline of Regulation NMS Implementation
Source: SEC

all-around winner in the post-Reg NMS world. Instead, through Reg NMS, the SEC has delivered a set of motivation for the introduction of Reg NMS. Ironically enough, this group may be the least impacted by the months of wrangling which has led to the current version of Reg NMS. Most individuals do not know anything about the Trade-Through Rule, nor would they be particularly interested in finding out. The SEC might have stood up for the silent majority, but in a real-world sense, there will be little if any impact on their way of investing.

- *Buy-side.* An ideal result of Reg NMS would have been abolition of the Trade-Through Rule altogether, as well as elimination of access fees. However, given the choice between DOB and TOB, most buy-side firms appear to be grudgingly satisfied with the latter option. However, without an opt-out clause, it is not the most ideal solution for buy-side firms who typically consider other factors in addition to price as a measurement for their best execution practices. The Trade-Through Rule certainly does not make things easier for those buy-side firms looking to move large block orders with minimum market impact. On the other hand, most buy-side firms appeared to be satisfied with the results of the Access Rule which essentially killed the ITS system in favor of private connectivity and mandated market centers, which will develop procedures to prevent locked and crossed markets.

- *Sell-side.* Similar to the buy-side, Reg NMS presents a mixed bag of emotions for the sell-side. In general, most would have preferred elimination of the Trade-Through Rule. However, given the choice between DOB and TOB, most went with TOB, with noticeable exceptions like Goldman Sachs. Although not many sell-side firms have agreed with the complicated calculations involved in market data revenue, the fact that they will be able to package their own data can be seen as a positive result. As the intermediary between the buy-side and execution venues, the sell-side will be asked to play a crucial role in complying with the various rules within Reg NMS.

- *Execution venues.*
  - *NYSE.* Given its precarious position in electronic trading, the NYSE got what it was asking for from the SEC, especially in terms of the TOB Trade-Through Rule. The DOB option would have been a devastating blow to the floor brokers and specialists. However, the long-term impact of Reg NMS on the NYSE is not clear. The introduction of the Hybrid Market was a reaction to Reg NMS. Although they will live to fight another day, the long-term effects of operating a hybrid

trading model are unclear. There is a very good chance that the order flow within the NYSE will be bifurcated, with liquid issues going to the electronic platform and the less liquid issues going to the floor. In the end, there is a very good chance (and a clear precedent in the European exchange market) that most of the order flow will migrate over to the electronic side. And once the order flow migrates over to the electronic platform, NYSE will have to compete against many credible competitors who have been entrenched in the electronic market for many years. As the NYSE opens itself up to true competition, it may find itself losing market share to its electronic competitors in the long run.

- *NASDAQ*. Despite the fact that NASDAQ did not get its wish to eliminate the Trade-Through Rule altogether, given its level of connectivity and historically low incidences of trade throughs, in the end, NASDAQ will be less affected by the final ruling than it initially appears. Building on its growing market share in listed stocks, NASDAQ may ultimately benefit from Reg NMS as it competes on equal footing against NYSE for additional market share in the exchange-listed market.

- *ECNs*. Similar to NASDAQ, ECNs would have been better off with the abolition of the Trade-Through Rule. If any form of trade-through were adopted, most would have also preferred the DOB option over TOB since it would have essentially eliminated the discrete liquidity (held by the floor brokers) which differentiates the NYSE floor from the rest of the electronic markets. The inflexibility of the capped access fee will not be a plus for the ECNs either. However, with their years of experience in the electronic markets, they will have a better chance to gain additional market share under the new Trade-Through Rule.

- *ATS*. Those ATSs in the block trading business should be quite happy with Reg NMS, which by extending the Trade-Through Rule to block trading has, in essence, made the institutional trading environment even more hostile to large block orders. Private block trading platforms, such as Liquidnet and ITG will become attractive alternatives for those buy-side firms looking for anonymity, speed, and liquidity. Although there is a certain level of uncertainty surrounding the lower market access threshold of 5%, it appears that given the business models of both Liquidnet and ITG, they would not have to abide by Reg NMS.

MARKET FRAGMENTATION VERSUS COMPETITION

The U.S. equities market has seen many ups and downs over the last decade. The market exuberance of the late 1990s has been met by uncertainty and stagnant growth. Fueled by ever-decreasing spreads, commission compression, and shrinking resources, both buy-side and sell-side firms have increasingly relied on electronic trading to both improve their productivity and to reduce costs. The high cost of execution is no longer acceptable to most buy-side firms. Perhaps more significant, however, is that a spirit of independence is gradually taking hold amongst the more sophisticated buy-side firms, especially given that the availability of trading technologies allows them more control over their trading activities.

The U.S. equities market structure has undergone major changes over the last decade. In the aftermath of the OHR of 1997, competition increased substantially, leading to the creation of various independent execution venues including ECNs and private ATSs. Market fragmentation appeared to be the norm, at least in NASDAQ, as various viable execution venues emerged to seriously threaten NASDAQ for execution revenues. Figure 2.9 displays the timeline of the U.S. market centers.

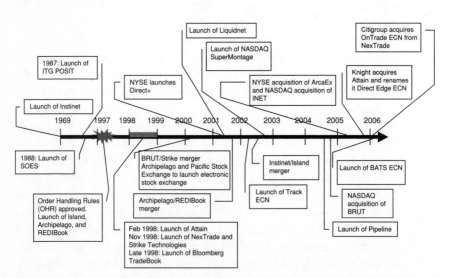

FIGURE 2.9 Timeline of the U.S. Equities Market Centers
Source: Aite Group

However, by 2002, a wave of consolidation began that was triggered by the merger between Archipelago and REDIBook (owned, at that time, by Goldman Sachs). The most significant ECN merger occurred when Instinet acquired Island (forming INET), its chief competitor in the ECN market. NASDAQ went on a spending spree soon after that, determined to recapture its lost market share by acquiring BRUT. This consolidation trend hit its peak when the NYSE acquired ArcaEx and NASDAQ teamed up with INET, thereby creating a de facto duopoly in the U.S. equities market. The conception and passage of Regulation NMS has also played a key role in recent market developments as new and incumbent execution venues look for opportunities in post-Reg NMS market structure.

The end result of all these M&A (Mergers and Acquisitions) activities was that in a short span of time, all of the large ECNs had disappeared, leaving the ECN market littered with smaller players. Perhaps more importantly, the NYSE and NASDAQ forcefully moved back to the top of the execution market. Figure 2.10 shows how the market consolidated.

Going against this industry trend of consolidation has been the acceleration of market fragmentation, at least on the surface. Since 2002, a number of ATSs, led by Liquidnet, have emerged to meet the growing need for block

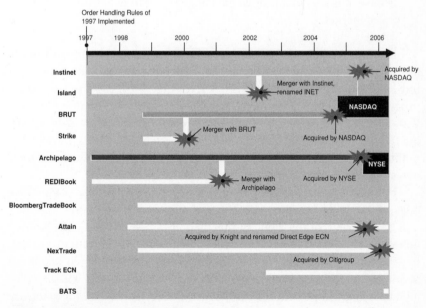

FIGURE 2.10   Market Consolidation
Source: Aite Group

trading in the marketplace. Fearful of total dominance by the NYSE and NASDAQ, large dealers and a number of buy-side firms have formed partnerships to either support existing regional exchanges or to create new execution venues. Large bulge bracket firms have also jumped into the fray by either launching or developing internal crossing engines designed to take advantage of the massive order flow going through their trading desks.

With the passage of Reg NMS and the resurgence of both the NYSE and NASDAQ, the future prospects of regional exchanges looked quite bleak. In the aftermath of the initial market consolidation, regional exchanges faced three realistic options:

- *Seek a partner.* One easy move would have been to merge with one another in the hope of creating enough liquidity and cost savings to compete against the larger players.
- *Buy or build an ECN/ATS.* Another option for a regional exchange was to buy an existing ECN/ATS or build one in the hope of creating a fully electronic exchange capable of competing in the post-Reg NMS market structure.
- *Move on.* Faced with insurmountable competition, regional exchanges could have ultimately shut down or could have sold their exchange license, perhaps to a foreign exchange trying to penetrate the U.S. equities market.

Instead, over the last 12 months, regional exchanges have come back to life, driven by investments from leading sell-side firms and, in some cases, buy-side firms. The Philadelphia Stock Exchange (PHLX) started the whole process by attracting investments from leading dealers. That was followed with an announcement from the Boston Stock Exchange (BSE) announcing the development of the Boston Equities Exchange (BeX), through the pulling in of investments from large dealers. Figure 2.11 shows a historical investment of market centers.

For all of the exchanges, the challenges to maintain their competitive edge will only get tougher in the age of sub-second executions. Latency will be the name of the game in this market that is driven by the need to adhere to the Order Protection Rule of Reg NMS. As the rate of messaging continues to increase in this trading arena, capacity could become a serious issue for a lot of the execution venues. Market data will also play an increasingly important role in the near future, as demand for extensive historical data as well as real-time data continues to grow, thanks to hedge funds and proprietary trading shops conducting black box trading.

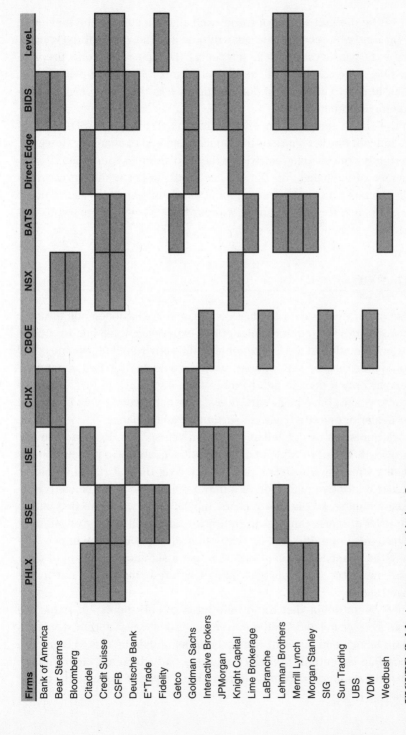

FIGURE 2.11 Investments in Market Centers
Source: Exchanges, ATSs, Broker/dealers

It will be difficult for all of these exchanges to survive the inevitable shake-up that will occur in the near future. For the regional exchanges, seeking external investments to jump-start their post-Reg NMS preparation has been the easy part of the overall strategy. Execution will be key, and their ability to attract additional liquidity into their platforms will determine their ultimate fate.

In the end, it seems inconceivable that the NYSE and NASDAQ could lose significant market share to the smaller regional exchanges. However, it is certainly conceivable that within the next three to four years, the total number of exchanges in the U.S. equities market could be down to four, at the most, from the current number of nine. Liquidity is the name of the game, and those exchanges without liquidity will be forced to exit the market.

DARK POOLS

The rise of dark pools over the last couple of years has been one of many changes that the U.S. equities market has experienced, leading to a complete transformation of the institutional trading environment. No one could have predicted that the U.S. equities market would go from two major market centers only a decade ago to more than 40 venues in 2009. Most of these new venues have been dark pools, whether owned by an individual broker/dealer or operated by a consortium or an exchange.

Dark pools can be defined as execution venues that do not to provide public quotes. The core value of a dark pool is its ability to provide access to liquidity while minimizing market impact. Over the last 12 to 18 months, this rather restrictive definition of a dark pool has been challenged as an increasing number of dark-pool users appear to be willing to live with a certain level of market impact in return for higher fill rates. Certain dark pools have also opted to link up with other dark pools in the hope of increasing the chances for client orders to get a significant portion of their orders done in the non-displayed market before being routed out to the displayed side.

There is no doubt that the proliferation of dark pools has made the life of an average buy-side trader extremely difficult, as real-time decisions must still be made in terms of where the order should be routed to get the best possible execution. In today's microsecond execution environment, market fragmentation certainly adds another layer of complexity to the buy-side.

Due to their "dark" nature, non-displayed pools are misunderstood by some, and downright distrusted by others. With increasing use of outbound and inbound indication of interests (IOIs) within certain dark pools, it is not currently clear whether the traditional definition of a dark pool still applies to a majority of the venues. One thing is certain, however: The overall market share of dark pools continues to grow, and regulatory intervention appears inevitable.

The non-displayed market is not a homogeneous one. One important note is that due to the variations in business models and target client base, dark pools do not necessarily compete against one another. A dark pool that focuses on facilitating buy-side block trading, for example, might link up with a dark pool that aggregates sell-side flow to add diversity in order flow. Similarly, broker-owned dark pools might link up with one another to increase overall fill rates for their collective clients. In fact, given the growing trend of dark pool linkages, coopetition (i.e., certain level of cooperation between entities that otherwise compete) has become more common in recent months. Broadly speaking, there are five different types of dark pools within the U.S. equities market: block trading dark pools, agency dark pools, consortium dark pools, exchange-operated dark pools, and internalization dark pools.

Block Trading Dark Pools

Led by industry pioneers like ITG POSIT, Liquidnet, and Pipeline, block trading dark pools seek to provide a trading environment in which large

TABLE 2.1 Block Trading Dark Pool

Platforms	Average Trade Size	Average Trade Volume	Institutional	Retail	Algos (algo-rithms)	Principal
Aqua	18,000	N/A	Yes	Yes	Yes	No
BlockCross	17,000	5 million	Yes	No	Yes	No
ConvergEx Cross	35,000	N/A	Yes	Yes	No	No
ITG Posit	6,000	24 million	Yes	No	Yes	No
Liquidnet	50,000	30 million	Yes	Yes	Yes	No
Pipeline	50,000	15 million	Yes	No	Yes	No

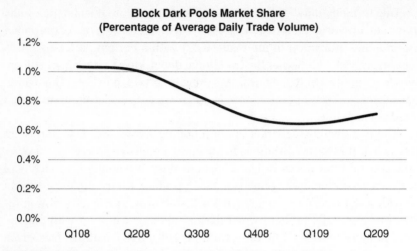

FIGURE 2.12 Market Share Trend of Block Trading Dark Pools
Source: Dark Pools, Aite Group

orders can be crossed with minimum market impact. Off-exchange block trading has always existed, and these block trading dark pools have flourished in recent years due to diminishing order size in the public market.

Even within the block trading dark pool category, business models vary widely. Liquidnet, for example, developed the passive trading model, in which blotters of their buy-side clients are constantly monitored to initiate negotiation-based execution. Under this model, the buy-side trader merely commits his or her uncommitted orders and waits for the contra to emerge. Under the more traditional active trading model, clients must actively enter orders or indications of interest to seek-out contra. Most leading block trading dark pools currently offer a blend of each trading model. Figure 2.12 shows the trend of block trading dark pools.

Agency Dark Pools

Operated typically by independent agency brokers, agency dark pools attempt to cross various client orders that flow through the broker. The key difference between agency dark pools and internalization dark pools is the fact that agency dark pools do not have principal interest in any of the executions. Due to the fact that there is a lack of principal trading involved, attracting client liquidity into these dark pools is not an easy feat. Most larger agency brokers, such as Instinet and ConvergEx, heavily involve their

TABLE 2.2 Agency Dark Pools (As of Q3 2010)

Platforms	Average Trade Size	Average Trade Volume	Institutional	Retail	Algos	Principal
ConvergEx VortEx	370	10 million	Yes	Yes	Yes	No
Instinet CBX	300	35 million	Yes	No	Yes	No
Knight Match	400	N/A	Yes	Yes	Yes	No
ConvergEx Millennium	275	20 million	Yes	Yes	Yes	No
SIG RiverCross	350	N/A	Yes	Yes	Yes	No
SunGard Valdi Liquidity Solutions	700	4 million	Yes	Yes	Yes	No

algorithms to ensure that extensive liquidity flows through their respective crossing platforms. Table 2.2 lists the major agency dark pools and Figure 2.13 shows the trend of market share of agency dark pools.

Consortium Dark Pools

Consortium-based dark pools such as LeveL and BIDS are typically owned by large broker/dealers and function as an industry utility. Execution costs also reflect consortiums' nature. LeveL has certainly thrived as an industry utility with an extremely aggressive pricing structure and attractive internalization feature for broker/dealers. Table 2.3 lists the two major consortium dark pools and Figure 2.14 shows the consortium dark pool market share.

Exchange Dark Pools

Major exchanges also operate dark pools, typically starting as point-in-time opening and closing crosses. The exchange dark pool approach has

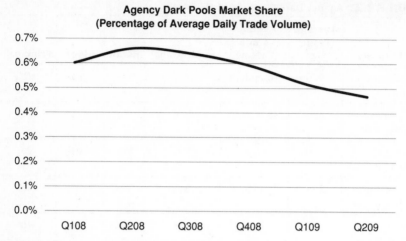

FIGURE 2.13 Market Share Trend of Agency Dark Pools
Source: Dark Pools, Aite Group

TABLE 2.3 Consortium Dark Pools

Platforms	Average Trade Size	Average Trade Volume	Institutional	Retail	Algos	Principal
BIDS	340	20 million	Yes	No	Yes	No
LeveL ATS	350	50 million	Yes	Yes	Yes	No

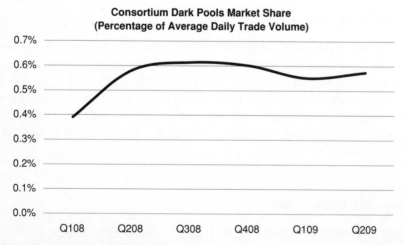

FIGURE 2.14 Consortium Dark Pools
Source: Dark Pools, Aite Group

TABLE 2.4 Exchange Dark Pools

Platforms	Average Trade Size	Average Trade Volume	Institutional	Retail	Algos	Principal
ISE MPM	250	9 million	Yes	Yes	Yes	No
NASDAQ Crossing	45,000	93 million	Yes	Yes	Yes	No
NYSE Match-Point	600	1 million	Yes	Yes	Yes	No

evolved with the introduction of continuous crossing options as well. The ISE's MidPoint Match (MPM) (now part of Direct Edge) presents the next stage in exchange operated dark pools through its fully integrated non-displayed and displayed environment. Table 2.4 lists the major exchange dark pools and Figure 2.15 shows the trend of market share in exchange dark pools.

Internalization Dark Pools

Definitely the largest of the dark pool category, internalization dark pool encompasses those broker-operated dark pools that *can* utilize their own

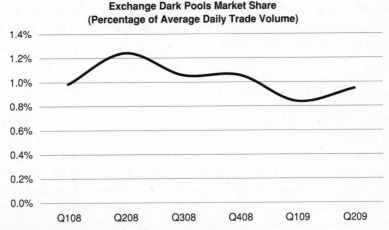

FIGURE 2.15 Market Share Trend of Exchange Dark Pools
Source: Dark Pools, Aite Group

TABLE 2.5 Broker Internalization Dark Pools (As of Q3 2010)

Platforms	Average Trade Size	Average Trade Volume	Institutional	Retail	Algos	Principal
Barclays LX	290	50 million	Yes	Yes	Yes	Yes
Citi Match	320	26 million	Yes	Yes	Yes	Yes
Crossfinder	279	229 million	Yes	Yes	Yes	Yes
GETCO Execution Services	320	100 million	Yes	Yes	Yes	Yes
SIGMA X	300	125 million	Yes	Yes	Yes	Yes
Knight Link	428	136 million	Yes	Yes	Yes	Yes
MLXN	N/A	N/A	Yes	Yes	Yes	Yes
MS Pool	229	54 million	Yes	Yes	Yes	Yes
UBS PIN	N/A	N/A	Yes	Yes	No	No

account to execute against client order flow. It is important to note that most of these platforms require that involvement of the dealer side be opted in by the clients. Those dark pools that involve market-making flow (such as Knight Link and GETCO) are part of this category. Table 2.5 lists the major broker dark pools and Figure 2.16 shows the market share of the broker internalization dark pools.

Key Trends in Dark Pools

Over the last decade, market fragmentation has become the norm in the U.S. equities market. This market evolution, coupled with huge leaps in available electronic trading tools, has certainly empowered the buy-side trading community. At the same time, market fragmentation has added much more complexity for the buy-side trader, especially as the market continues to move toward a sub-second trading environment. The lack of standardized information regarding each dark pool certainly has not helped the buy-side's cause either.

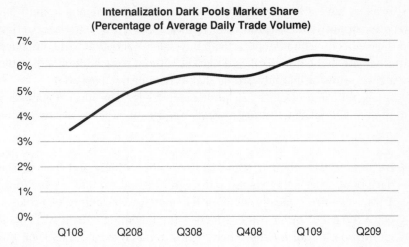

FIGURE 2.16 Market Share Trend in Broker Internalization Dark Pools
Source: Dark Pools, Aite Group

On the other hand, the major broker/dealers have benefitted over-all from the growth of dark pools for many reasons. Most major broker/dealers currently operate their own dark pools. This is because, as an increasing percentage of client orders get crossed in their own internal dark pools, execution costs go down. In addition, developing an internal crossing platform has enabled many of these firms to centralize their key client flow (e.g., institutional, hedge fund, retail, etc.) into a single location, achieving much-needed efficiency in their overall operations. Finally, market fragmentation has enabled broker/dealers to remain key partners of the buy-side even as their buy-side clients continue to take more direct responsibilities over their trading activity.

Indication of Interests, Immediate or Cancel orders, and Liquidity Mapping

Nothing in life stays static, and the dark pool market is no exception. What started out as an island, touting diversity of unique internal and customer flow and cost-effective, low-market-impact execution service has now evolved to something much larger and more connected, leading to the current market reality in which many of the dark pools are now connected with each other as well as with displayed markets.

Brokers have also developed algorithms (algos) designed to sniff-out execution opportunities within various dark pools. These dark aggregation algos have become quite popular with buy-side traders that feel compelled to participate in the non-displayed market without truly understanding the unique workflow or liquidity profile that exists in each dark pool.

Along with increasing dark pool connectivity, the market has seen adoption of IOIs as a means to growing crossing rates. There are two types of IOIs:

- *Inbound IOIs.* Inbound IOIs are used more widely and lead to the dark pool order being routed out to an external venue for execution. These IOIs are typically handled by smart order routers of brokers. Once the smart order router receives the incoming IOIs, it will check its own dark pool for the other side. If a match exists, the order will be sent away via the smart order router to be executed at an external venue.

- *Outbound IOIs.* A more controversial version of IOIs—outbound IOIs—requires the dark pool to transmit profiles of existing resident orders (i.e., symbol, side, size, or price) to external liquidity sources to attract the other side into the dark pool for execution. The only firms that publicly acknowledge this functionality are Liquidnet, NYFIX, and ISE. None of the internalization dark pools have claimed use of outbound IOIs. Given the fact that there are many more venues that actually accept inbound IOIs (again, typically through their smart order routers) than outbound IOIs, one must assume that outbound IOIs are more widely used than actually reported.

In addition to IOIs, another source for potential information leakage within the dark pools is usage of IOC (immediate or cancel) orders. Inbound IOCs are more common than outbound IOCs as there is a much higher probability of information leakage for outbound IOCs, as these orders have no guarantee of being executed and could leak specific trading intentions to outsiders.

Another burgeoning area of interest within the dark pool market is the liquidity mapping functionality being developed as part of brokers' smart order routing technology. In the traditional smart order routing world, routing decisions are mostly made by real-time, quote-driven information. In order to better navigate through the non-displayed pools, an increasing number of brokers have created sophisticated liquidity mapping tools that can provide real-time statistical predictions in terms of routing options among the various dark pools.

From a post-trade analysis perspective, certain brokers also offer analysis of execution quality against specific order flow type for customers (i.e., execution quality against retail flow versus proprietary flow). This way, customers can continue to fine-tune their dark pool strategies and avoid interacting with specific order flow types that might no longer be beneficial.

Growing Presence of High Frequency Flow

Growing market presence of the high frequency trading community in the U.S. equities market has been well covered in recent months.[1] Traditionally, high frequency participation in dark pools was quite minimal at best as the lack of reliable price discovery mechanism made it almost impossible for data-driven high frequency trading firms to commit to dark pools. In recent months, however, high frequency trading firms have surfaced as a major liquidity source in various dark pools.

One of the main reasons for their participation is the fact that the overall growth of the dark-pool market made it hard for high frequency firms to simply ignore participating in these pools. In addition, aggressive execution costs offered by some of the dark pools have made it attractive for high frequency participation. Availability of dark pools' performance data—which drives liquidity mapping features—has also helped in attracting high frequency flow.

Efforts by a few of the dark pools to focus on drastically lowering their latency appear to validate this trend of growing high frequency participation. While it is too early to truly gauge, there is no doubt that the growing presence of high frequency flow has played a vital role in the overall increase of dark pool market share over the last few quarters.

Calls for Regulation

During the last 12 months, a call for tighter regulation has become the norm. Given its dark nature, the often misunderstood dark pool has been

---

[1]For Aite Group coverage on high frequency trading, please refer to the following Aite Group reports: "New World Order: The High Frequency Trading Community and Its Impact on Market Structure", February 2009, and "High Frequency Trading: A Critical Ingredient in Today's Trading Market", May 2009.

one of the areas that has gained close regulatory scrutiny. That said, Aite Group believes that an outright ban on dark pools is highly unlikely considering the level of dark pool presence in the U.S. equities market. Potential dark pool regulations include the following:

- *Standardization of reporting.* Dark pools are not currently required to publicly share any volume data. Certain dark pools double-count all of their volume, even if the order was actually executed externally. Other dark pools double-count what they cross on their own platform, and single-count volume that they route out. Standardizing reporting standards should provide a much better view into the actual size of the non-displayed marketplace.
- *Use of IOIs and IOCs.* IOIs and IOCs have helped certain dark pools gain significant market share in recent months. Regulators have voiced concerns over the growing use of IOIs and IOCs, at times, equating them to quotes that would certainly cause issues with the existing rules on Regulation ATS and Regulation NMS. If regulators ultimately decide to implement tighter control over dark pools, IOIs and IOCs will certainly be two of the major issues to be addressed.

Another area of discussion for the regulators has been the potential of lowering the threshold for fair access under Regulation ATS from today's 5% to between 1% and 2%.[2] The threshold being lowered would certainly create a natural ceiling, restricting the growth of dark pools moving forward.

Focus on Anti-Gaming Functionality

As dark pools have become more popular, the potential for predatory behavior has also increased. Sensing trading opportunities against unsuspecting institutional liquidity, a growing number of firms have engaged in predatory trading behaviors (e.g., stock price manipulation by constantly

---

[2]The Five Percent Rule states that ATSs registered as broker/dealers, displaying quotes to subscribers and trading in excess of 5% of the average daily volume of a national market stock in four of the preceding six months are required to submit quotes to a national securities exchange or NASD for distribution to market data vendors.

pinging with small orders to discover larger size in the dark pool). Buy-side concerns over growing potential for gaming in dark pools have led to heightened efforts by the broker/dealers to develop sophisticated anti-gaming features built into their platforms. Dark pools have created various automated trading surveillance features to detect any suspicious trading patterns. In addition more flexibility has been built into the platform so that the customers can set specific parameters around potential order interaction with the dark pool (i.e., setting a price, size, volume, frequency, or market cap limits for potential crossing).

Growth of Dark Pools

Despite the growing notoriety of dark pools in the public, adoption of dark pools has increased unabated. One difficulty of estimating the growth of the dark pool market is the fact that there are no volume reporting standards that all dark pools follow. Aite Group's past projections on dark pool market share had been driven by conflicting volume figures that more often than not double-counted volume reported by specific dark pools while single-counting the consolidated market volume. In this Impact Report, all volume data has been single-counted to ensure consistency.

Of the 27 dark pools interviewed for this report, 26 dark pools agreed to be profiled. Of the 26 dark pools profiled, 19 provided average daily trade volume. Not all of the 19 dark pools provided historical average daily trade volume.

Aite Group estimates that dark pools account for approximately 13% of the U.S. equities market as of Q1 2010. There is a chance that the 13% estimate is a conservative number, given that it is based on incomplete volume data. Select interviews with large broker/dealers seem to indicate that the actual market share of the dark pool market is more than 20%. Figure 2.17 shows the estimated market share of dark pools based on a daily average trade volume.

This uncertainty stems from the fact that about 13% of the trade volume is being reported to the Trade Reporting Facility (TRF). Some of the broker/dealers interviewed for the report assume that the volume figure accounted for by the TRF also represents dark pool volume. Unfortunately, without better reporting requirements, the actual size of the dark pool market remains nothing more than an educated estimate at this point. Figure 2.18 breakdowns the U.S. equity market share by venue type.

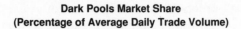

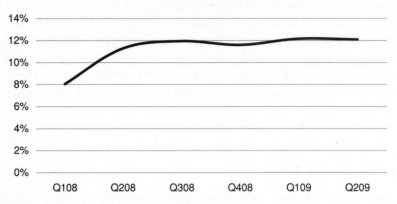

FIGURE 2.17 Estimated Market Share of Dark Pools
Source: Dark Pools, NYSE Euronext, NASDAQ OMX, Direct Edge, BATS Exchange, Aite Group

Looking at the market share of dark pools by types, internalization dark pools represent the largest category, at 70% of the market. Exchange dark pools account for 11% of the market, followed by block dark pools at 8%. Figure 2.19 shows the market share of dark pools by category.

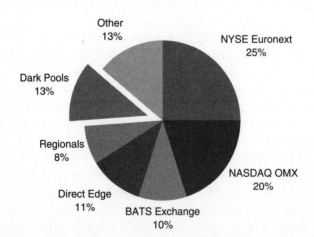

FIGURE 2.18 U.S. Equities Market Share by Venue Type as of Q1 2010
Source: Dark Pools, NYSE Euronext, NASDAQ OMX, Direct Edge, BATS Exchange, Aite Group

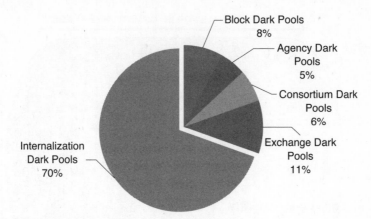

FIGURE 2.19 Market Share of Dark Pools By Category as of Q2 2009
Source: Dark Pools, Aite Group

Defining the Role of Dark Pools

The evolution of the dark pools market continues. The initial focus of dark pools providing alternative venues for facilitating block trading has transformed into a dynamic marketplace with diverse business models and technology innovations. For the active users of dark pools, the trade-off between the potential for information leakage and increased chances for a fill must be carefully considered. This simple, yet crucial consideration will ultimately help determine the losers and winners in the dark pool market.

Figure 2.20 illustrates a snapshot of dark pools analyzed by potential for information leakage, average daily trade volume, and average trade size. One important thing to note is that this diagram is a snapshot representation only as the dark pool market appears to be in constant flux.

Firms considering the use of dark pools should ask the following questions:

- *What type of order flow will I be interacting with?* Investigate the type of order flow (i.e., institutional, retail, proprietary, etc.) you can interact with in the crossing platform, and ask if periodic performance measurement can be provided per type of order flow that you ultimately interact with. In addition, make sure that you can opt out of interacting with specific order flow that you do not want to trade against.
- *Do you use IOIs and IOCs? If so, how?* Remember that IOIs and IOCs are not, by definition, "bad." While you might risk a certain degree of

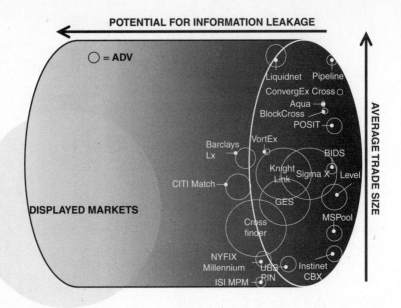

FIGURE 2.20 Dark Pools in Snapshot—2009
Source: Dark Pools, Aite Group

information leakage in using them, use of these tools might also increase your chances of getting a fill. Before jumping to conclusions, examine each dark pool's policy toward IOIs and IOCs. If IOIs and IOCs are used, ask for detailed workflow to ensure that information leakage is minimized.

- *Do you link with other dark pools? If so, how?* Ask questions about how the dark pool is linked up with other dark pools, and the exact workflow behind how orders or trading intentions are conveyed to other dark pools. Most brokers currently provide access to other dark pools via their dark pool algos and not necessarily directly from their dark pools. Also ask about the type of liquidity mapping expertise that the broker has developed to ensure that your order is being routed to other dark pools properly and not randomly.
- *What kind of anti-gaming functionality have you built into the dark pool?* The potential for abuse in the dark pools has naturally increased as the market share of dark pools has grown over the last few years. Make sure that the dark pool is taking an active approach; this will help ensure that information leakage does not lead to opportunities for predatory traders.

CHAPTER 3

Trading Infrastructure

I ncreased reliance on electronic trading and algorithmic trading, combined with regulatory and structural changes, accelerated the pace of overall electronic trade messaging rates over the last few years. These trends are, perhaps, most notable in the United States, but are clearly the direction for global markets as well; these trends are not just in equity but in all exchange-traded products. The near quadrupling of U.S. equity messaging volumes since December of 2006 is a clear indicator of the scale of this increase. Figure 3.1 shows the growth in TAQ (trade and quote) data.

If U.S. equities continue their pace, Aite Group expects message volumes to average 1.2 billion messages per day by 2011. The market already saw peak days approaching this number in late 2008. Electronic trading firms should expect to have to manage those rates on a consistent basis while accounting for new peaks that could approach 1.8 billion messages per day on high days. Few, if any, existing market data infrastructures could sustain those data levels as they exist today.

Options pricing is exponentially worse than equities market data volumes. Current Options Price Reporting Authority (OPRA) data peaks exceed 1 million messages per second. Aite Group expects OPRA will generate peaks exceeding 2.2 million messages per second by the end of 2010. Figure 3.2 shows the OPRA growth rates.

The trend of exponentially growing data volumes is putting tremendous stress on existing infrastructure in the front offices of global investment banks as well as their actively trading customers. The high-performance trading infrastructure that exists today is primarily

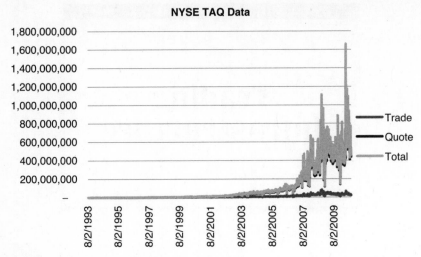

FIGURE 3.1 Exponential Growth in TAQ Data
Source: NYSE Euronext, Aite Group

composed of various technologies: data normalization, complex event processing (CEP) engine, messaging software, and distributed cache. Combine these with high-performance databases and grid computing functionality with advanced applications on top, and a clear picture of the modern trading infrastructure begins to emerge.

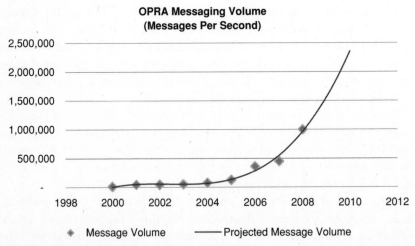

FIGURE 3.2 OPRA Growth Rates
Source: OPRA, Aite Group

RISE OF HIGH PERFORMANCE TECHNOLOGY VENDORS

The evolution of the modern trading-desk infrastructure is very much a function of the confluence of market factors that are driving transaction levels to extremes. The main factors include the adoption of electronic trading, the rise of algorithmic trading, the rise of alternative investment strategies, regulatory changes, and increased market fragmentation. Many of these trends are most evident in equities, but are appearing, to different degrees, in other emerging electronic asset classes.

More than any trend, the rapid rise of electronic trading has created an environment of greater ease in incorporating strategies that require greater and greater frequencies of trading. It is clearly evident that the volume of trading increases as electronic trading becomes more accepted in a more and more electronic market. Many sell-side firms that have increased their algorithmic offerings as a response to this trend find that their legacy infrastructures are not up to the challenge of the stresses that these offerings place on them.

As firms began to dissect the situation looking for areas of improvement, several themes became apparent. Consolidated data managed by data aggregators was far too slow to create competitive algorithms. This led to the challenge of looking to bring direct exchange and venue feeds into a firm. This created considerable difficulty in maintaining the data infrastructure, as each exchange and venue has unique data formats that had to be translated to properly communicate with internal systems. This trend ultimately led to the rise of third-party feed handlers to properly normalize data introduced into trading firms. This trend has played out greatly; today, many of the choices that some sell-side, and many on the buy-side, are looking at service offerings that yield low-latency data in a less resource-intensive fashion.

Another part of the trading infrastructure that began to stress under the increasing load was the messaging infrastructure. Much of the software that was in place in various firms included proprietary messaging, transport software, or vendor solutions, which have introduced significant latency into the trading infrastructure. This trend has yielded a class of ultra-fast messaging software that has grown up in the financial services or has been transported from other industries, where speed was critical.

Concurrently, firms have had to develop greater means of storing and sharing disparate data across many systems. This type of data sharing can occur across a single trading infrastructure or across a global trading infrastructure, as is the case in many of the largest investment banks.

Many of the latency issues that the most latency-sensitive firms have experienced are not issues for all types of firms. Firms battling in the sub–25-millisecond realm of algorithmic and strategy trading have different requirements than other types of firms. However, many of the challenges that the most speed-sensitive firms face can become issues for other types of firms as massive messaging rates overwhelm trader workstations, profit/loss (P/L) engines, analytic engines and, particularly, the order management systems at certain firms. That being said, there are many firms that operate with consolidated data as their main engine of data for a myriad of systems.

Some of the key drivers for increased messaging volume and pressure on overall trading infrastructure include the following:

- *Rapid adoption of electronic trading.* Electronic trading has become the de facto medium for order entry and trade executions. The adoption of electronic trading has moved into other asset classes in recent years as traders look to electronic trading as a competitive necessity. Figure 3.3 displays electronic trading adoption estimates for multiple asset classes.
- *Growing adoption in algorithmic trading.* Similar to electronic trading adoption, firms have moved beyond equities in terms of algorithmic trading, applying automated trading strategies to various asset classes, including options, FX (foreign exchange), and fixed income. Growth of algorithmic trading has also expanded into other global markets. Figure 3.4 displays estimates of the growth in algorithmic trading in multiple asset classes. Figure 3.5 displays estimates of global expansion of algorithmic trading.
- *Implementation of Regulation NMS and beyond.* The continued implementation of Regulation National Market System (Reg NMS) has had a far reaching impact in the U.S. equities market, especially in terms of institutionalizing electronic trading. Reg NMS has created a new environment for competition as new players and incumbents struggle for growing market share in the U.S. equities market.
- *Market fragmentation.* A trader looking for execution in the U.S. equities market currently faces more than 40 potential execution venues. The use of intelligent smart-order routing and robust data infrastructure plays a key role in this fragmented market reality.

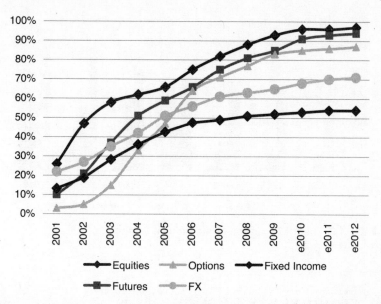

FIGURE 3.3 Adoption of Electronic Trading
Source: Aite Group

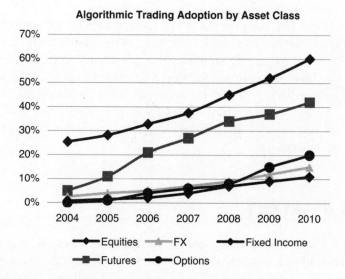

FIGURE 3.4 Growth in Algorithmic Trading
Source: Aite Group

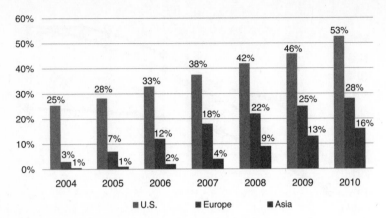

FIGURE 3.5 Global Expansion of Algorithmic Trading
Source: Aite Group

KEY COMPONENTS OF HIGH PERFORMANCE INFRASTRUCTURE

Figure 3.6 shows a high-level schematic of some of the key components of the modern high-performance trading infrastructure.

One of the key components of the modern high-performance trading infrastructure is the messaging software. Additionally, there are some hardware-based messaging solutions that are beginning to emerge, such as Tervela. Another important feature of this overall space is the reliance by firms on a variety of vendor solutions. It is beginning to be quite common to see a combination of a CEP engine, distributed cache, and grid-computing solution all sitting on top of a common messaging bus for a given trading desk.

FEED HANDLERS

Associated with new liquidity points, feed handler creation and maintenance have been a challenge for most firms. More than three-quarters of the firms we spoke with write their own feed handlers, which support feeds from multiple liquidity points and data providers. Every tier-one firm and most tier-two firms we spoke with supported redundant data feeds for backup, often augmenting direct feeds with a consolidated provider.

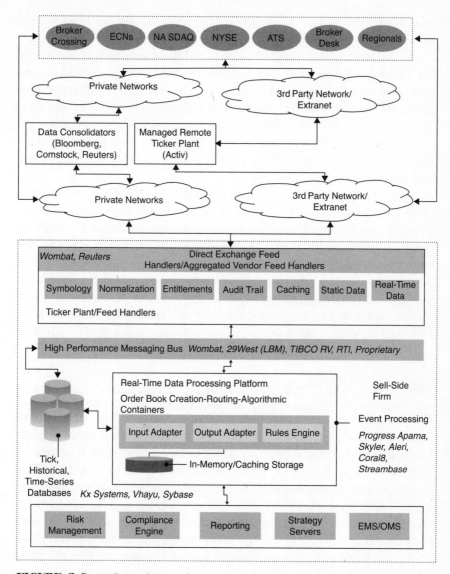

FIGURE 3.6 High-Level View of High Performance Trading Infrastructure
Source: Aite Group

In addition to back-up data, electronic trading inherently requires a hot/hot failover system receiving the same data. Coupled with downstream integrations, feed handlers can support more than 100 data streams at some firms

Firms that choose to write their own feed handlers typically cite a competitive advantage in speed. Even so, the process can be challenging. One European firm spoke about the poor documentation provided by emerging MTFs on connectivity. Several other firms mentioned internal code as the frequent source of latency bottlenecks. While firms may feel internal development creates a competitive advantage over third-party providers that may not always be the case.

Most feed handlers support equities data, which is often the most understood data for technical staff that lack domain expertise. As firms move into other asset classes, growing and maintaining a library of internal handlers could prove difficult and ultimately costly if internal handlers are not benchmarked against commercial products available to the general market. Across the firms Aite Group spoke with, feed handlers required 2.5 full-time equivalent engineers to build and support. If the average fully loaded compensation for a good engineer is US$200,000, that adds up to US$500,000 per firm per year in building and maintaining feed handlers.

TICKER PLANT

Feed handlers are only one component of the ticker plant. Ticker plants have been an evolving landscape the last few years. First, there was the bidding war for Wombat (won by NYSE Euronext). Next, IBM bought Infodyne. Thomson Reuters has been adding new feeds to their Data Feed Direct product. QuantHouse, FTEN, and other trading providers have augmented their services with market data capabilities. Lastly, hardware acceleration is on the radar for several of the providers to compete with hardware-accelerated commercial products already on the market. All of this technology innovation comes with a price. One tier-one firm we spoke with pays US$7 million per year in license and maintenance for their commercial ticker plant. Add the dozen full-time employees required to support the infrastructure to the cost, and that firm is paying close to US$10 million per year. Another tier-one player we spoke with built their own ticker plant, and maintains it with 10 full-time employees.

Those costs and infrastructure requirements are relegated to the largest firms. Smaller firms have smaller costs, but can wind up having to engage in burdensome tasks as a result. One hedge fund, for example, has a team of three managing their market data infrastructure, which must rotate cleansing duties every night. It takes them between one and one-and-a-half hours to make sure they have accurate prices for high, low, close, and bars for their models.

Another firm told us the vendors all do a good job, but they would like to buy a solution that performs with more functionality. In order to supply more breadth, several ticker plant providers are moving into the middleware space.

MESSAGING MIDDLEWARE

Queuing issues with messaging middleware are driving firms to evaluate a myriad of innovative new options. In fact, this was the most active area of infrastructure change among firms with whom we spoke. While they maintain a significant market share in generic technology stacks, TIBCO and IBM face an increasing array of competitors in the electronic trading space, and those competitors come from diverse backgrounds.

Exchanges and liquidity access providers like QuantHouse and NYSE Euronext have implemented their own messaging middleware for client access. NYSE Technologies wrote their own middleware using Remote Direct Memory Access (RDMA) to bypass the operating system, and create a shared memory approach. Each processing node runs its own *daemon*, or background process, to manage fan-out capabilities of the messaging infrastructure. NYSE Technologies claims they can push 2.1 million 200-byte messages in 700 nanoseconds point-to-point on their middleware, though NYSE Euronext supports other middleware providers. QuantHouse built FeedOS, their proprietary middleware, to move market data through their infrastructure. Customers access the middleware through client-side application programming interfaces written in Java, C++, or C#. Internally, FeedOS is C++ running on a Linux 64-bit architecture. QuantHouse wrote FeedOS to be natively multi-threaded, allowing them to scale up to new hardware as it becomes available. In fact, they are currently working on a field-programmable gate array (FPGA) instance to run the OPRA feed in a hardware appliance.

Beyond exchanges, trading firms are implementing a variety of solutions to solve messaging infrastructure challenges. Two firms we spoke with implemented solutions that originated in the defense industry. The first firm implemented Real-Time Innovations (RTI) after an evaluation of other leading vendors. The firm found all to be similar in performance, but

RTI offered lower "jitter" (where latency becomes less variable under load and when the network is having issues). The firm had previously built everything internally, and required an extensive benchmark. By moving off of internally developed solutions, the firm hopes to see economic benefits from not having to keep growing their server farm to support rising volumes. RTI also offered out-of-box management tools that their internal solution could not perform, freeing them from an additional management headache. The firm also needed to free-up resources, given that one of their largest internal challenges in this area is hiring.

RTI leverages a messaging protocol called the data distribution service (DDS). Expect to hear a lot more about DDS and the advanced message queuing protocol (AMQP) over the next year or two from standards groups and vendors. These two standards will battle it out, each hoping to become the default messaging protocol in low-latency trading infrastructures. There are advantages and limitations to both, and Aite Group expects neither will achieve the goal of becoming a de facto standard.

Another technology firm moving beyond defense into capital markets is PrismTech. PrismTech founders came from Thales, the French defense contractor, where they wrote the messaging systems for naval vessels. PrismTech's OpenSplice DDS has only acquired one customer in capital markets thus far: a high-frequency trading firm on the West Coast.

Like many firms in this space, that firm prefers to write their own technology. They were going to write their own middleware as well, but decided to select OpenSplice after an evaluation of several vendors. Similar to the NYSE Euronext architecture, OpenSplice leverages a central daemon on each processing node to create shared memory architecture. The product does not behave like a traditional publication/subscription model, instead creating shared memory databases and moving data between each database. In fact, while the customer likes the product, they admit to not being a fan of DDS as a standard. The firm has ten traders and six engineers, and needs all of them focused on building quality algorithms rather than middleware. They also collocate their entire infrastructure. OpenSplice is currently only leveraged for trade reporting, but the firm has plans to move in inside mission-critical trading applications based on its performance.

A fixed income department at a tier-one firm took the shared memory concept in a different direction with a solution that originated largely from the health care industry. InterSystems Caché replaced messaging between a pricing group and a collection of traders where latency was in the seven to ten second range. Instead of looking at various middleware platforms for messaging, the firm decided to improve latency in this instance by implementing a request/response architecture against a data caching solution. By implementing the solution against a high-performance database, they were able to solve their reporting requirements as well as aggregate market data from multiple sources.

Perhaps the most well known messaging specialist in electronic trading, 29 West, came up as either part of an existing infrastructure or as one of the vendors in an evaluation for many of the firms interviewed. Their product, Latency Busters Messaging (LBM), received praise from several firms for its simplicity and stability. On the flip side, one firm told us they feared selecting 29 West because they thought the company had grown so much they might become another TIBCO or IBM and let their performance wane. When we asked 29 West about this directly, they expressed a commitment to stay focused on messaging. Further, when approached recently to enter the feed handler business, 29 West deferred to other vendors.

Speaking of TIBCO, feedback on their Rendezvous product was less than stellar. TIBCO hopes to combat their decline in the market with a new instance of Rendezvous running on Solace hardware. The hardware appliance ran at one existing client through its beta testing, and went live in February of 2009. The appliance is built on FPGA architecture, but uses a transmission control protocol (TCP) connection between the client and the Rendezvous daemon. TCP can be difficult to maintain during peak message volumes. The good news for TIBCO customers is the client protocol from legacy Rendezvous to the appliance version did not change, so servers can be exchanged for appliances.

Tibco's marriage to Solace Systems' hardware is an odd co-opetition, given that Solace offers dedicated market data distribution solutions of their own. Other hardware messaging providers gaining traction include Tervela (mentioned previously) and IBM, which have discussed porting their Infodyne acquisition to hardware. For pure market data, Exegy, Redline Trading, SpryWare, and Celoxica also provide hardware solutions. Aite Group expects hardware-accelerated middleware to gain significant traction in low-latency environments. Right now, the message is speed. At average data rates, hardware versus software is a relatively moot point. Hardware distinguishes itself during peak volumes by remaining consistent in its delivery and being less susceptible than software platforms to jitter. More than half of the firms we spoke with had implemented or were evaluating hardware-accelerated solutions.

The overlooked benefit of hardware is the amount of rack space firms can reduce for market data distribution. Firms we spoke with saw at least ten to one reductions in the servers required to perform the same tasks. If firms are paying US$15,000 a month for a collocated rack, space can be at a premium. So, while list price on some of these solutions may seem high, the vendors as a collective group have not done a very good job articulating an accurate cost/benefit analysis to the industry. Aite Group has seen competing software solutions that, at price per node, more than match the cost of a hardware solution.

STORAGE

Market data volumes tax more than real-time infrastructures. With regulatory requirements from MiFID (Markets in Financial Instruments Derivative) and Reg NMS, firms are required to store five and seven years of order data and Level 1 data to prove best execution. Beyond regulatory requirements, many firms store as much Level 1 data as they can acquire for backtesting purposes. For large firms with multi-asset global trading operations, that storage requirement can add up to their needing 2.5 petabytes of capacity for 2009 data alone.

Even equity-only firms can encounter increasing capacity restraints. Storing all current Level 1 and Level 2 data for U.S. equities is approaching a three terabyte a month requirement.

While storage requirements are highest for equities and options, other asset classes require capacity planning as well. In 2006, one hedge fund was storing 75 megabytes of data per day. Today, that firm stores 350 megabytes per day on average, which more than doubles storage requirements on an annual basis

All of this storage can add up. With the exception of one small proprietary trading firm, every firm we spoke with used a storage area network (SAN) to retain their market data. The trading firm uses a connected storage device with capacity to add serial advanced technology attachment (SATA) drives as they need more capacity. The solution is relatively inexpensive, but impractical for all but the smallest firms.

Instead, most firms employ SANs to provide access to the data throughout their network for risk, compliance, back-testing, and other reasons. On top of the SAN, roughly one-third of the firms we spoke with wrote their own capture and storage for market data. Another third leverage

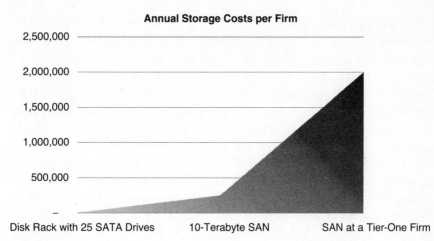

FIGURE 3.7 Storage Costs
Source: Aite Group

structured databases from Oracle, Sybase, and others. Remaining respondents leverage software from Vhayu and Kx. Between physical storage and associated software, costs can range from less than US$10,000 to US$2 million annually. Figure 3.7 shows estimated storage costs.

NETWORKING

Network configurations pose their own challenges with market data. Improper network configurations are one of the top latency issues according to one of the leading latency monitoring providers. Firewall configurations, turning Internet protocol (IP) routing on, fan-out problems with providers, and other issues all cause problems with market data infrastructures. Beyond the configuration problems, cost can be a problem. Given that distance between hops is the number one latency issue, and with market data volumes continuing to grow at a torrid pace, firms have had to increase bandwidth ratios on capacity planning for peak messages per second. One 45-megabyte Digital Signal Level 3 (DS3) point-to-point can run tens of thousands of dollars per month.

Because of cost and maintenance, networking is one area firms are offloading. Colocation for market data is growing in popularity as the industry heads toward dense connectivity.

COLOCATION

Driven by the ever-increasing need to mitigate latency, colocation has become a popular option for high frequency trading shops. Locating their optimized market data and actual trading models at or near data centers hosting exchange matching engines can shave off precious microseconds.

Pricing structure related to colocation is a straightforward per month, per rack charge; however, the actual pricing varies widely, ranging from as low as US$1,500 per month to more than US$10,000 per month, depending on location, type of service (i.e., simple real-estate rental vs. total managed service), and availability of other value-added services. One overlooked variable in the overall pricing structure is the enormous amount of power often needed to maintain an effective colocated infrastructure. Any potential clients of colocation services should definitely inquire about potential added costs associated with power usage. Figure 3.8 shows Colocation cost estimates.

Colocation provides users with the lowest possible latency to particular execution venues, as well as a certain level of resiliency from occupying the same physical location as the execution venue, by eliminating potential failure points such as various external connectivity and networks. The potential downside of colocation is high cost and the reality of a single point of failure that now exists outside of one's firewalls in a remote location.

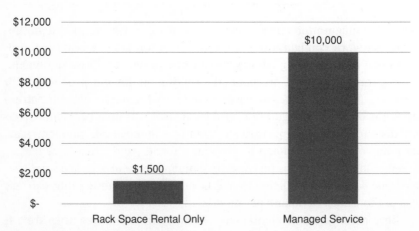

FIGURE 3.8 Colocation Costs
Source: Aite Group

Unlike the exchanges of the past, which typically owned their own data center infrastructure, most rapidly growing ATSs (alternative trading systems) have opted to host with third-party data centers. As a result, data centers have been battling over the privilege of hosting these new execution venues, which in turn makes it much easier to win new colocation clients that are looking for the shortest physical distance to multiple, highly liquid execution venues. Savvis's data center in Weehawken, New Jersey, for example, hosts both BATS and NYSE Arca and is a hotbed for colocation business.

SPONSORED ACCESS

Sponsored access has many different meanings for market participants, and, while widely talked about, is often misunderstood. The origin of sponsored access can be traced back to the practice of direct market access (DMA), in which a broker who is a member of an exchange provides its market participant identification (MPID) and exchange connectivity infrastructure to a customer interested in sending orders directly to the exchange. In this way, the broker has full control over the customer flow, including pre- and post-trade compliance and reporting. The DMA customer, in turn, gains direct access to major market centers. Figure 3.9 displays a direct market access workflow.

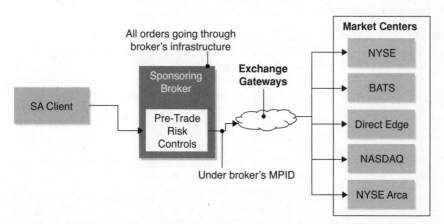

FIGURE 3.9 Direct Market Access Workflow
Source: Aite Group

While DMA can theoretically be considered part of a wider definition of sponsored access, Aite Group proposes a more restricted definition of sponsored access for the purpose of this report. We define sponsored access as a non-member entity (i.e., a sponsored participant) gaining direct access to market centers by using the MPID of a member broker/dealer (i.e., sponsoring brokers), leveraging access infrastructure not owned by the sponsoring broker.

There are potentially three types of sponsored participants in a sponsored access arrangement:

- Broker/dealer that is a member of the market centers
- Non-member, registered broker/dealer
- Non-broker/dealer organization

Table 3.1 shows the type of participants in sponsored access.

Firms opt to go through a sponsored access arrangement for many different reasons. While reduction in latency is one of the factors, other, more basic reasons include additional revenue opportunities and hitting volume discounts.

TABLE 3.1   Type of Sponsored Participants

Type	Motivations for Participation
Member broker/dealer	— Lower execution costs by piggybacking off a member broker/dealer's volume discounts — Higher rebates
Non-member broker/dealer	— Lower execution costs by piggybacking off a member broker/dealer's volume discounts — Gain direct access to market — New revenue source for attracting customers looking for direct market access — Higher rebates — Anonymity
Non-broker/ dealer entity	— Lower execution costs by piggybacking off a member broker/dealer's volume discounts — Gain direct access to market — Anonymity — Subject to less regulation and costs

Sponsored access models prevalent in the U.S. cash equities market can be divided into two specific types based on whether real-time risk checks exist at an account level. These are:

- *Filtered sponsored access.* More conventional and widely accepted by bulge bracket firms and third-party vendors, this model allows the sponsored participant to gain direct access to market centers via a dedicated port provided by the sponsoring broker. Risk controls and connectivity are typically provided by the sponsoring broker's recommended third-party vendors or service bureaus. The sponsoring broker can set up and monitor pre-trade risk parameters, and, if necessary, remotely modify and/or shut down trading activities. Figure 3.10 displays the workflow for filtered sponsored access.
- *Unfiltered sponsored access.* Also known as "naked" access. Under this sponsored model, the sponsored participant gains direct access to the market centers via a dedicated port provided by the sponsoring broker, but lacks real-time pre-trade risk monitoring by the sponsoring broker. Instead, the sponsoring broker receives post-trade drop copies of each

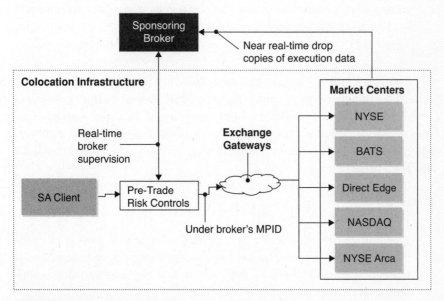

FIGURE 3.10 Filtered Sponsored Access Workflow
Source: Aite Group

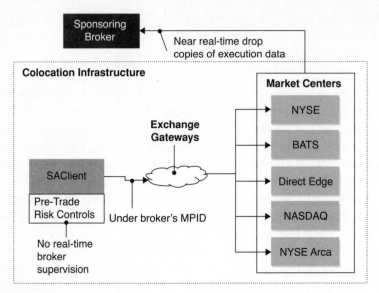

FIGURE 3.11 Unfiltered Sponsored Access Workflow
Source: Aite Group

transaction, which may or may not be received in near real-time and may or may not be used for any type of position risk management. Figure 3.11 displays the workflow for unfiltered sponsored access.

The term "filter" in this instance does not imply actually filtering orders for single-order quantity or price, but refers to the sponsoring broker's capability to provide real-time risk checks at an account level. In this scenario, real-time risk checks do not obtrusively filter, but unobtrusively monitor the flow. Intervention is triggered only when a position limit has been breached.

Several key characteristics help define today's sponsored access business:

- Technology infrastructure that supports sponsored access is not provided by the sponsoring broker because their current systems are centralized. A robust colocation infrastructure is required in order to support today's high frequency trading needs.
- Colocation increasingly plays a vital role in overall sponsored access relationships, and is especially attractive for market centers looking to gain additional order flow and revenue sources.

TABLE 3.2 Types of Pre-Trade Risk Checks

Type	By Exchange Ports	Order Across Venues	By Sponsored Account	Ability of Sponsors to Stop Participant Order Flow
Market Center	Single	No	No	No
Third-Party/ Broker	Across Ports	Yes	Yes	Yes
Fund Risk Checks	Across Ports	Yes	Yes	No

- Conceptually, a tri-party relationship exists between the market center, sponsoring broker, and sponsored participant, all through contractual agreements.
- The ultimate legal, financial, and reputational risk of managing a sponsored access arrangement lies with the sponsoring broker.
- Each sponsoring broker must perform due diligence on prospective customers looking for sponsored access; however, there is no standard, industry-accepted checklist for sponsoring brokers.
- Three potential types of pre-trade risks are involved in sponsored access.
- Market center-provided, port-level, pre-trade risk controls that check for order-level restrictions vary depending on the venue, and feature different latency levels. The main weakness of this approach is its being completely siloed into a particular venue only. As such, it lacks the ability to check across venues and by account.
- Lack of sponsoring broker-provided, pre-trade risk controls does not automatically mean that sponsored participants do not have their own sophisticated pre-trade risk filters. In fact, some of the sponsored participants are sophisticated proprietary trading firms with broker/dealer licenses. Despite this, the sponsoring broker does not ultimately have the ability to control the sponsored participant's order flow in real time.
- The third-party-with-a-broker-supported-pre-trade risk model tries to bridge the strengths of the first two pre-trade risk approaches, enabling checks across venues and by account. It also provides the flexibility to monitor and change the sponsored participant's order flow in real-time if necessary.

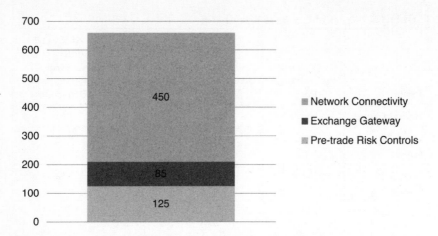

FIGURE 3.12 Average Latency Per Sponsored Access Component (in Microseconds)
Source: Market centers, broker/dealers, vendors, high frequency trading firms, Aite Group

There has been a lot of focus on the need for ongoing latency reduction to gain competitive edge. When breaking down the key sponsored access infrastructure components, network connectivity typically accounts for a significant portion, with an average of 450 microseconds. Exchange gateways add another 85 microseconds, and the industry average for typical pre-trade risk checks accounts for approximately 125 microseconds, with per-risk checks averaging anywhere from five to ten microseconds. Figure 3.12 shows an estimate of the average latency per sponsored access component.

Latency levels across the three often-used types of market access vary widely, leading to a potential competitive edge for those firms able to achieve ultra-low-latency trading infrastructure. For traditional DMA service, industry average currently ranges from four to eight milliseconds. For colocated, filtered sponsored access, the latency level dips into microseconds, ranging from 550 to 750 microseconds. Unfiltered sponsored access, not surprisingly, has the lowest range of latency, with 250 to 350 microseconds. Figure 3.13 shows an estimate of the average latency per sponsored access type.

There are many different reasons for the growth of sponsored access usage. The most obvious market driver has been the adoption of high

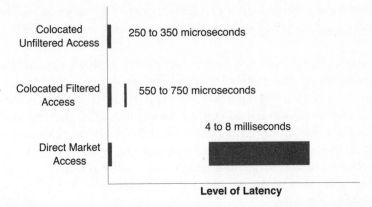

FIGURE 3.13 Estimated Latency Per Sponsored Access Type
Source: Market centers, broker/dealers, vendors, high frequency trading firms, Aite Group

frequency trading. The overall growth in high frequency trading is directly correlated with increased use of sponsored access. High frequency trading currently accounts for close to 70% of the average daily trading volume in U.S. equities, with a significant percentage of high frequency volume coming via sponsored access arrangements.

Sponsored access has many benefits to be gained by the parties involved:

- For high frequency trading traders with robust risk management capabilities, it enables dramatically faster access to market centers.
- Benefiting from volume aggregations services from the likes of Wedbush, Penson, Fortis, and Newedge, small to mid-size brokers can now compete on a level playing field with the larger brokers. This allows them to hit the maximum volume tiers and capture attractive pricing points across EDGX, NASDAQ, and NYSE Arca.
- From an additional revenue perspective, revenue-sharing arrangements between sponsoring brokers and sponsored participants that are also registered brokers can be beneficial for both parties involved.
- Exchanges benefit from additional liquidity into their venues to boost volume and revenue. In addition, market centers operating their own data centers can expect additional revenue from value-added services such as colocation.

Sponsored access, on the other hand, has specific risks and challenges for participating parties as well as for the market overall. These include:

- Supporting non-filtered sponsored access can lead to sponsored participants taking unacceptable levels of risk, which can cause both great financial burden and reputational damage to the sponsoring broker.
- In order to support non-filtered sponsored access, sponsoring brokers must develop strong risk management and due diligence teams capable of handling sponsored participants' credit and operational risk.
- Broker-to-broker sponsored access can lead to a situation in which the sponsoring broker loses track of the activities of the sponsored broker's customer.
- Providing filtered sponsored access often leads to a higher pricing point for sponsored participants, leading to favorable competitive conditions for those brokers offering unfiltered sponsored access.
- While potential is slim, there is a chance that a rogue sponsored participant can increase overall systemic risk.

Sponsored access (i.e., both filtered and unfiltered sponsored access) trading volume accounts for 50% of overall average daily trade volume

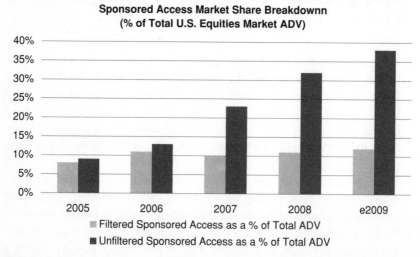

FIGURE 3.14 Estimated Breakdown of Filtered vs. Unfiltered Sponsored Access
Source: Market centers, broker/dealers, vendors, high frequency trading firms, Aite Group

in the U.S. equities market. Analyzed separately, the market share of filtered sponsored access currently stands at 12% of total average daily trade volume, whereas the market share of unfiltered sponsored access currently stands at 38% of total average daily trade volume. Figure 3.14 breaks down the market share of filtered and unfiltered sponsored access in U.S. equities.

CHAPTER 4

Liquidity

L oosely defined as the ease with which a market can facilitate buyers and sellers of securities with minimum level of friction, liquidity is the foundation of the capital market. Not so long ago, liquidity providers in the equities market were regulated market makers and specialists, who were legally bound to market two-side markets and provide liquidity into the market in exchange for access to market information that gave them an advantage over other market participants.

However, with the rapid adoption of electronic trading and democratization of available market information, the role of traditional liquidity providers has changed drastically. In fact, the concept of traditional market makers and specialists no longer has a strong footing in the U.S. equities market. In the overall evolution of the equities market structure, high frequency traders are often viewed as the next generation liquidity providers.

HFT AS LIQUIDITY PROVIDERS

Electronic markets need electronic market makers; there is no other way of displaying tradable prices other than through an algorithm. Standing in front of a freight train of buyers or sellers is not an easy endeavor. Liquidity providers are not in the business of losing money and if the rules are changed to impede the potential of making profits, the amount of tradable prices will decline and the bid/offer spreads will widen. This debate will continue but the reality is the cost of trading will increase for all market participants. Unfortunately there are trading days that are outlierrs that put the subject of market making into the main stream of life. The year 2010 had such a day and May 6th 2010, will be a day to remember.

FLASH CRASH

The price charts of 2010 will contain a day that many chartists that view it in the future will consider an anomaly. The hope of the entire financial market industry is that it will indeed be a one-time occurrence. It is never a pretty sight to watch a market selloff. In 1987 when the stock market had its worse percentage one-day loss, the feeling that many had that day was one of complete helplessness. Program trading was the target for blame that day and automated trading has now been blamed in 2010.

The immediate reaction to the selloff was to assume that a trading error had taken place. The so called fat finger error was relatively common when electronic trading first started, but many advances have taken place with pre-trade risk management to avoid such an occurrence. This is not to say that there are not still many firms that do not practice such policies and this is where and why the regulatory community needs to be able audit any firm that actively trades.

So what really happened that day? The first thing to understand in the months prior to May 2010, was that the equity markets rallied significantly without many down days. This uptrend was broken in the weeks before May 6th. Many trading participants and their strategies involve trend following. The equity markets were very vulnerable to a selloff. The markets may have rallies or declines based on technical reasons or simply put, the position of the speculative accounts. If speculators are leaning one way, the market can experience violent moves as they liquidate their positions. This can be from the long or short side, as many short squeezes have propelled markets higher. The NASDAQ bubble in the early 2000s is a prime example of a market moving in a direction without a fundamental backdrop. As a market is making this kind of move, the so-called market pundits will always try to justify a market's reaction. Of course when a market is moving higher and the public is profiting there is little or no discourse.

Understanding the market's position is vital to understanding why the flash crash happened. The overall market was already under pressure due to the credit crisis in Greece. Then at 2:42 PM eastern, with the Dow Jones Industrial Average down more than 300 points for the day, the equity market began to fall rapidly dropping more than 600 points in five minutes for an almost 1000 point loss on the day by 2:47 PM. Twenty minutes later, by 3:07 PM, the market had regained most of the 600-point drop. Reports of massive put buying on the S&P (standard and poor's) index, large selling of e-mini futures, and selling of the Euro currency versus multiple other currencies were all reasons for this market failure. When all of these bearish trades hit the market at the same time, panic set in and there were not enough buyers to handle such flows. All of the indexes did retest the flash crash lows within the month and later in July when the market went below these levels again. As frightening as the day was, there was vindication for the automated trading community. Since then the regulators have concluded that automated traders were not manipulating the market and in fact the ones who stayed in the market help prevent a further collapse, in addition to the fact that they also had one of their most profitable days of the year. Fundamental decisions by individual money managers were behind the flash crash, there are many problems with the equity market structure that exacerbated the situation and they hopefully will be corrected in a rational way.

Circuit breakers have now been implemented across many single name securities. This a good start as no established companies' stock should trade at a penny. The ten percent limit may be too tight as the chances of market manipulation increases with such a tight limit. . Halting a single name security while allowing the overall index to continue to trade, forces firms who provide liquidity to make assumptions about the price of the halted stock as opposed to letting it continue to trade. This is why circuit breakers have not been used previously as they actually create more uncertainty in certain circumstances. As always there is no perfect solution as there will always be risks in the trading of any asset class or security.

Eliminating stub quotes will be the easy thing to do as why any venue would accept an order that has no value to the market is puzzling. Certain single names traded at a penny, because the order books on the buy side of the market were all taken out. This leads to an order type issue, as anyone who uses stop orders should be required to put a limit on the order. Using market orders does have its risks and all retail and institutional traders are now fully aware.

The market-making obligation issue is a complicated one as the venues must incentivize market makers to stay in the market. As stated earlier, market making is a for-profit business and even if market makers are required to stay in the market, they will never agree to be in a market 100% of the day, unless they have attractive incentives to do so.

Market fragmentation in the equity market is also partially responsible for the flash crash. The amount of venues that one can trade has reached a major saturation point. Although competition has benefited the market in certain ways, specifically the reduction in trade cost, having multiple venues with different technology and rules in order, handily, can cause mayhem when the market is in a panic mode. On May 6th certain exchanges were slow in acknowledging orders which forced many liquidity providers to pull out of the market. Uncertainty in regards to trade cancellations also will add to the confusion for market makers as they are hesitant to trade when there is a question as to whether the trade they entered will be allowed to stand.

May 6th will remain as a reminder of the risks inherited in investing and trading. Whether you are a retail or institutional investor the marketplace is filled with danger. When markets are going higher and the majority of the population is making money, automated trading is an afterthought, when the reverse happens the criticism will continue. For those in the industry and for those who plan on entering, make sure you have thick skin. Let's hope an event like May 6th does not happen again, but do not bet on it.

CHAPTER 5

Trading
Strategies

W here do the ideas for trading strategies come from? The idea that automated trading came from traders that never were involved in the market is not true. Although the majority of actual developers of automated trading systems never traded in their lives, the strategic minds behind the modelers came from the world of manual traders. From either the exchange trading floor or from one of the many trading desks of financial institutions, the ability to profit from trading is one developed from over years of experience. High frequency trading (HFT) is all about making profits in short time frames with as minimal risk as possible. The key to a short-term trading strategy is the trading data that comes out of each day's trade. It does not matter if it is an equity, currency, bond, or a derivative. Each market is about matching up buyers and sellers and how one can interpret the price action in the most efficient way. Those who can will be the ones who are the most successful.

Analyzing the top of the book is the first step. The top of the book is defined as the current bids (buys) and offers (sells). As an example: If the current market is 10.50 at 10.51 with 1,000 on the bid (10.50) and 10 on the offer (10.51) the logical assumption would be that since the bid is much larger than the offer the next trade would be more likely to be at 10.51 than 10.50. This is not a guarantee since there may have been a trade done prior that sold at the price of 10.51 that took all the bids out at 10.51 and left an extra 10 to be offered at 10.51. The next moments will tell the story: Will the amount to be sold at 10.51 increase or will the bid at 10.50 change or will there be a trade at either price that will change the scenario yet again? Imagine calculating the above price action in one's mind over and over again in multiple markets in multiple listings. In the manual trading era a market specialist would watch a few listings or markets and make the appropriate decisions. Automated trading now allows one to watch and trade multiple listings/markets and hopefully make profits.

Not all the action takes place at the top of the book; most strategies will monitor the depth of the book as well. The depth of the book is defined as the amount of securities/shares available to buy and sell at prices below the top level. As the previous example shows, the market is constantly updating, so any trading strategy should know and remember what is available at different price points over the period of the day, weeks if not years. This daily price action may not seem important to a long-term investor, but the constant trading that takes place every day provides price discovery to all participants.

The number of trading strategies is endless and the most effective are those that have only been recently developed. The life span of a strategy varies, but although the core aspect of data mining will be essential, you will need to constantly update your strategy to remain ahead of the competition.

Outside of the previously discussed strategies of market making and statistical arbitrage, momentum trading is another common strategy. Used to make small profits as well as a way of establishing longer-term positions, momentum traders have no fundamental basis and will go long or short and even reverse positions. Prior to the electronic trading boom, momentum traders were originally chartists or technicians. The art of studying charts has been in the business of trading for many years. This was the original way of detecting what insiders were doing with their orders. Watching the tape has now evolved into the electronic world of trading by traders looking to buy or sell breakouts of markets that are in a consolidating mode.

A correlation strategy is another example, it can be defined in many ways, but is mainly a statistical relationship between two or more variables such that systematic changes in the value of one variable are accompanied by systematic changes in the other. The premise in trading is to find out what contract leads and what other contract follows. One can purchase or sell a Canadian index, for example, after the U.S. index moves in any direction. This strategy is used for trading all asset classes.

Basis trading is an HFT specialty. The basic definition of the basis is the difference between the price of a commodity or asset in the cash market ("spot price") and its price in the futures market. It is a market for the broker and professional trading community, and has gravitated to the HFT trading area, where point-and-click traders have no chance to compete. Connectivity to the major inter-dealer cash platforms is necessary.

News-event-driven trading is gaining popularity as event-based algorithms search for key words or phrases in news releases that can potentially move markets. This type of strategy is still evolving; risking capital on a news story that may be incorrect or misleading can be risky.

EXAMPLES OF ALGORITHMS

The act of sending an order for execution in an electronic marketplace is facilitated by algorithms. Not only are HFTs using them, but the majority of buy-side institutions employ them as well. There is a plethora of third-party vendors who supply algorithms as well as many sell-side brokers who develop their own for their customers. Some are complicated and others not, but trying to execute orders without any price slippage and information leakage is the goal.

The basic suite of algorithms that are readily available include the volume weighted price average (VWAP), timed order entry (TWAP), pegging to the bid or offer, and arrival price. There are many other types of algorithms that are slight derivations of the most used algorithms. The basic suite is used across the different asset classes. A description of these follows:

- *VWAP*: This is computed from a beginning cut-off time to an ending cut-off time, and is calculated by volume weighting all transactions during this time period.
- *TWAP*: The goal is to achieve the time-weighted average price calculated from the time you submit the order to the time it completes.
- *Pegging*: A pegged order is designed to maintain a purchase price relative to the national best offer (NBO) or a sale price relative to the national best bid (NBB).
- *Arrival Price*: This attempts to achieve the bid/ask midpoint price at the time the order is submitted, taking into account the user-assigned level of risk aversion which defines the pace of the execution, and the user-defined target percent of average daily volume.

ORDER TYPES

Not to be confused with an algorithm, order types are the gateway to the marketplace. The two typical orders are market and limit. Market orders are filled at the best bid or offer, often dangerous in volatile markets, most institutional customers will avoid them and always put a limit price on their orders. Limit orders do have risk as well, as a trader can spend time chasing the market to get them filled. So the best advice is for a trader to use limits but to make sure you are selling below the best bid and buying above the best offer to guarantee a completed trade. Stop orders are also popular with the trading community as they in theory protect a trader's existing position. They also are used to enter a position as many chartists will only want to enter a market if a certain price point is breached. Buy or sell stops have to have an accompanying limit price or they can be market orders once the price point is hit. As an example: A trader can use a buy stop at 100 for stock ABC with a limit of 101. When the stock trades at 100 the buy stop will turn into an order to buy at 101 or better. If you use a market price you will be filled at the next price best offer in the market. Sell stops are the same with a stop price below the current market price.

There are many other advanced order types. Table 5.1 describes some of more common ones.

TABLE 5.1 Order Types and Descriptions

Order Type	Description
IOC	Immediate or cancel: Order fills as much as possible and then cancels the balance.
FOK	Fill or kill: Order needs to be completely filled or it will cancel the order completely.
Iceberg	Hidden size order type: Adds additional size to an order as it gets filled, and can be the same order size or a random amount.
Trailing Stop	Stop price adjusts as market moves.
MIT	Market if touched: Order is converted into a market order when a certain price point is breached.
MOO	Market on open: Order is executed at market price when the market opens.
MOC	Market on close: Order is executed at market price within one minute of market closing time.

FLASH ORDERS

The flash order controversy is one of the more interesting examples of fierce competition between the trading venues for order flow. How does a venue increase volume and market share? Outside of lowering fees and offering volume discounts, a venue can create a new order type that caters to a certain client. A flash order is one that allows a trader to advertise their willingness to trade at a certain price point. Other participants can then respond to this by showing how much they are willing to trade without the trade being offered to other trading venues. This style of trading was accepted by the industry, but it came under the spotlight when other exchanges complained about its exclusivity. The issue became a larger story when Politian's intervened on the behalf of their constituents. The options market is now also embroiled in the same issue as the traditional option exchanges allow the same sort of order type. It is more commonly known as a step up order. This order is used to allow market makers to increase the size amount of their bids and offers to match the desired amount of options that they are willing to trade.

HIGH FREQUENCY TRADING AND PREDATORY STRATEGIES

When it comes to high frequency trading strategies the goal has always been to create a model that can calculate mathematical probabilities in the shortest time frame possible. HFT strategies are proprietary and extremely valuable. There have been multiple cases of indictments against employees who have left their firms with proprietary codes. Trading firms need to protect their intellectual property. In December of 2010 Sergey Aleynikov, formerly a programmer at Goldman Sachs, was found guilty by a New York jury of stealing trade secrets and transporting stolen property. Aleynikov left Goldman to work at Teza Technologies and was convicted of stealing high-frequency trading software. He is scheduled to be sentenced March 18 2011 and faces as much as 15 years in prison. The idea of predatory strategies is one that will continue for as long as the markets remain electronic. Order anticipation strategies are used by all high frequency traders, who are takers of liquidity as well as the ones who provide liquidity. Trading will always reflect supply and demand principles; in addition attempting to anticipate the price direction of any security will remain part of the markets. This does not guarantee profits as the growth of electronic trading has actual leveled the playing field. Are high frequency traders who try to take advantage of others who are less sophisticated a detriment to the market? The answer will depend on who is answering the question. There will continue to be conspiracy theories as long as money is involved.

CHAPTER 6

Expansion in High Frequency Trading

FUTURES

High frequency trading (HFT) in the futures markets is not a new development. Once the markets started to go electronic—in the mid-1990s in Europe and in the early 2000s in the United States market participants (a majority of them ex-floor traders) quickly realized that they would need to translate their trading style from a pit environment to an electronic platform style in order to stay competitive. Pit trading was all about watching the trading flow and how much size was on the bid and to offer when the price point changed, and electronic trading is no different. Live market data needs to be consumed at a rapid pace to predict future price movements, and the ensuing trade decision needs to be made as quickly as possible. Other types of traders use similar ways of accessing the markets, but their time horizons can last longer. As such, the high speed trading market has two silos: a liquidity provision model that is dominated by professional proprietary trading shops, and a model-based, customer-driven order flow that uses execution algorithms to enter and exit positions. Approximately 25% of overall major global futures volume is derived from professional high frequency traders. This trend is only expected to increase as additional professionals for other asset classes gravitate to futures and increase participation for other developing nations around the globe. Model-based,

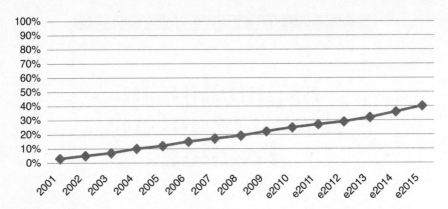

FIGURE 6.1 Professional High Frequency Trading Firms' Percentage of Volume in the Futures Markets 2001–2015—Estimated
Source: Aite Group

customer-driven order flow represents approximately 60% of the amount of orders generated in the futures markets. This percentage will also continue to increase as the point-and-click order entry style of order entry will not be able to stay competitive. The exchange landscape will continue to be driven by technology upgrades to trading platforms and improvements in the ability to deliver real-time market data. A new entrant will arrive in 2010 as the NYSE Liffe U.S. part of the NYSE Euronext family of exchanges plans on entering into the U.S. interest rate futures market. The exchange will need to offer something new, as multiple copycat markets have failed to bring liquidity to their markets. Providing some type of margin savings to real end-users of futures is the only way of gaining any real market share. Upcoming regulatory changes will not change the primary regulator, but the potential prospect for mandates to trade standardized over-the-counter securities on an exchange-type platform may bring an unexpected windfall to the futures exchange. Figure 6.1 shows an estimate of the market share of professional HFT trading firms

Current Landscape in Futures Markets

The futures markets continue to be dominated by electronic execution, given that the only futures contracts executed by the pits today are related to options trading. Further, the options markets have been slow to adapt to electronic trading, mostly due to the difficulty of streaming prices

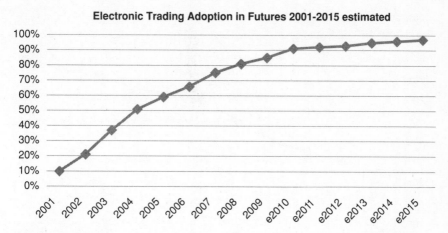

FIGURE 6.2 Electronic Trading Adoption in Futures 2001–2015—Estimated
Source: Aite Group

on complex multi-leg option strategies. In the long-term, the futures and option markets will become completely electronic. Figure 6.2 shows the electronic trading adoption in the futures markets.

Order Generation Proprietary Trading

The futures markets were originally created for commercial hedgers, which led to other financially based contracts being created to hedge interest rates, currency, and equity risk. As in any trade made to offset risk, a third party needs to be part of the transaction: the speculator. Although speculators are now being demonized by politicians, regulators, and the general public, there would be no market without them; matching up two end users on the opposite sides of a transaction is a very difficult job. The original liquidity providers, commonly known as "locals," would stand around a pit and provide a bid/offer spread to market participants. When the markets went electronic, the world that they were used to changed dramatically, and the players had to adjust. Gone was the edge that a pit environment provided, and no longer were they able to see the eyes of the brokers who filled orders for the large institutions. Short-term traders that traded for a tick or tried to buy the bid and sell the offer all day, commonly known as "scalpers" were now faced with the prospect of converting their trading style to an electronic marketplace. This led to the birth of

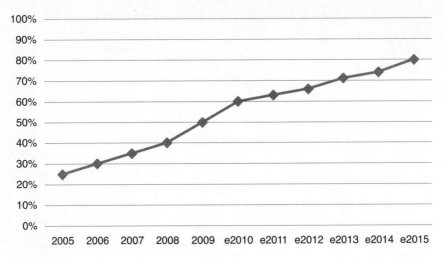

FIGURE 6.3 Algorithmic Model-Based Order Generation in Futures 2005–2015—
Estimated
Source: Aite Group

high frequency trading in the futures markets. Floor traders adjusted, and
the smartest ones started their own proprietary trading shops to provide
liquidity and trade futures, hiring quantitative experts to create trading algorithms that used various trading strategies. Figure 6.3 shows an estimate
of the amount of orders being generated by algorithmic models.

FIXED INCOME

The fixed-income markets trade treasury on the run (latest issued), off
the run (older government issues) bonds and notes, corporate bonds,
agency bonds, repurchase agreements (repos), municipal bonds, mortgages, and many different types of derivatives. The most common fixed-
income derivative is the interest rate swap and the most controversial is
the credit default swap. For years voice execution dominated all aspects of
fixed income. In the early part of the last decade, electronic trading started
to appear in the active treasury complex (2 year, 5 year, 10 year, 30 year).
The trading style of the broker dealer platform community was never a simple matching of buyers and sellers. The cash treasury market has a style of
trading called "work up." This is where an existing bid or offer is traded on
and then other traders can join the trade to increase the amount of bonds

or notes transacted at the original price point. High frequency traders are very active on these types of platforms as well as multiple brokers who have automated order generators that use the same type of technology as HFTs.

Traditional buy-side traders execute their interest rate trades through their prime broker or through one of the many buy-side requests-for-quote-type trading platform. Multiple brokers/dealers provide the liquidity on such platforms. Most of the risk is then transferred to other traders in the interdealer market who are using HFT technology. The on-the-run treasuries volume being generated by HFTs is estimated to be approximately 35% to 40%.

Since many of the OTC (over-the-counter) treasury products that are considered standardized will now be mandated to trade electronically the HFT community will continue to look to expand their presence in such markets. Where the trades get executed is still an open question, as the regulators have yet to decide what the rules will be for the competing platforms in the space. HFTs need to get historical market data information and also gain access to such platforms for them to have any impact on liquidity.

FOREIGN EXCHANGE MARKET

While regulatory scrutiny continues to build in the U.S. equity market driven by populist-led political pressures, high frequency trading has expanded well beyond the cash equity market. Over the last eight years, one area of expansion has been in the thriving foreign exchange (FX) market.

Key Market Trends in Foreign Exchange

After robust market growth in 2007 and 2008, the global FX market experienced lower volatility, lower volume, and in most cases, wider spreads. Large banks pressed on, maintaining the global FX market's overall market dominance, while the FX ECN (electronic communication network) market witnessed declining market share. At the same time, the retail side of the market continued to see increased adoption despite market consolidation and the threat of additional regulations. This section of the report discusses a few of the key market trends and statistics impacting the FX market today.

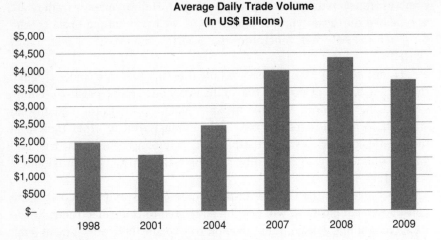

FIGURE 6.4 Trends in Global FX Volume
Source: BIS, Bank of England Foreign Exchange Joint Standing Committee (JSC), New York Foreign Exchange Committee, Singapore Foreign Exchange Market Committee, Canadian Foreign Exchange Committee, Tokyo Foreign Exchange Joint Standing Committee, and Aite Group

Global Foreign Exchange Market Volume Estimates

Thanks in large part to high volatility, 2008 yielded historical highs in terms of overall trading volume, followed by an inevitable decline in 2009. The industry averaged approximately US$4.3 trillion in daily trading volume in 2008 compared to about US$4 trillion in 2007. During the latter part of 2008 and well into 2009, customers faced a much different market from previous years, marked by wider spreads and declining liquidity. Consequently, average daily trade volume returned to earth in 2009, standing at approximately US$3.7 trillion. Figure 6.4 shows the trend in global FX volume.

Adoption of Electronic Trading

Unlike other OTC markets, driven by early acceptance in the interbank market, electronic trading adoption continues to increase in the global FX market. Given that markets remain fragmented, the need to source multiple liquidity pools simultaneously has only strengthened the overall position of electronic trading. At the end of 2009, electronic trading accounted for approximately 65% of all FX trading. This figure is expected to reach

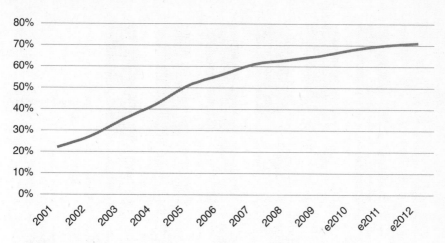

FIGURE 6.5 Estimated Adoption of Electronic Trading in FX
Source: Aite Group

more than 70% by end of 2012. Figure 6.5 shows the estimated adoption of electronic trading in foreign exchange.

Bank Internalization

Another key trend over the last few years has been the increasing effectiveness of large FX banks in managing their risk books when trading against customers. By utilizing sophisticated pricing engine and real-time internalization capabilities, large FX banks have become quite adept at showing varying prices to different types of customer segments as well as efficient at deciding when to internalize versus utilize traditional interbank markets to lay off their risk. In a way, the aftermath of the credit crisis of 2008 has only reinforced banks' need to internalize, particularly as regulators and politicians continue to emphasize banks' need to lower their overall risk profile. Consequently, the need to better segment customer flow has been on top of banks' overall client-facing trading strategy so that they can optimize their balance sheets and better manage their profit and loss (P&L).

Increasing Presence of Client-to-Dealer Market

As banks continue to fine-tune their ability to manage their FX risk books in real-time, the client-to-dealer market has increased its overall market share over the last few years at the expense of the interbank market. By

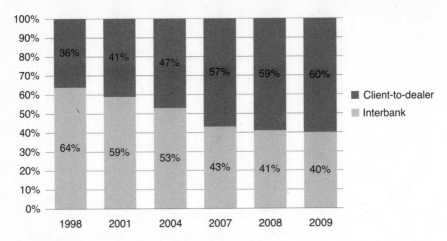

FIGURE 6.6 Client-to-Dealer VS. Interbank Market
Source: BIS, Bank of England Foreign Exchange Joint Standing Committee (JSC), New York Foreign Exchange Committee, Singapore Foreign Exchange Market Committee, Canadian Foreign Exchange Committee, Tokyo Foreign Exchange Joint Standing Committee, and Aite Group

the end of 2009, the client-to-dealer market accounted for approximately 60% of overall FX trading while the interbank stood at 40%. In comparison, the interbank market represented close to 60% of the marketplace in 2001. Figure 6.6 compares the client-to-dealer market to the interbank market.

Examining the interbank market, led by the dominant presence of Reuters and EBS, electronic trading has clearly become the preferred method of trading, accounting for 70% of all interbank trading. Figure 6.7 shows the breakdown of voice versus electronic execution in the interbank market.

On the other hand, voice trading still remains a vital part of the client-to-dealer market. In fact, voice trading actually increased during the latter parts of 2008 and 2009, as market uncertainty and wider spreads forced customers to deal directly with their FX banks. At the end of 2009, electronic trading represented 43% of the client-to-dealer market. Figure 6.8 displays the breakdown of voice versus electronic execution in the client-to-dealer market.

Historical Look at High Frequency Trading in FX

While the banks have gone through a series of consolidations, leading to fewer banks making markets, the FX market continues to evolve with new

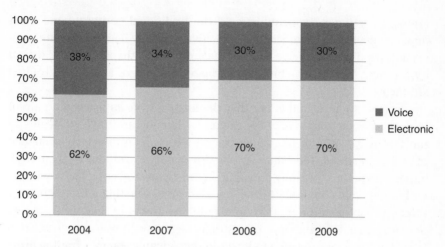

FIGURE 6.7 Electronic Trading in Interbank Market
Source: BIS, Bank of England Foreign Exchange Joint Standing Committee (JSC), New York Foreign Exchange Committee, Singapore Foreign Exchange Market Committee, Canadian Foreign Exchange Committee, Tokyo Foreign Exchange Joint Standing Committee, ECNs, and Aite Group

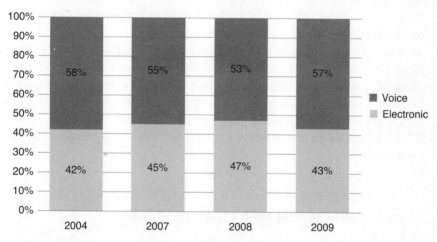

FIGURE 6.8 Electronic Trading in Client-to-Dealer Market
Source: BIS, Bank of England Foreign Exchange Joint Standing Committee (JSC), New York Foreign Exchange Committee, Singapore Foreign Exchange Market Committee, Canadian Foreign Exchange Committee, Tokyo Foreign Exchange Joint Standing Committee, ECNs, and Aite Group

types of customer segments beyond the traditional corporate and asset manager customer base. Since 2002, actively trading hedge funds and proprietary trading firms have made a huge impact in the FX market, driven by a robust IT infrastructure and the development of automated trading strategies.

In fact, some would argue that the large FX banks learned a painful lesson between 2002 and 2006, driven by latency arbitrage strategies in the first wave of high frequency trading firms. As a direct consequence of this experience, the banks initiated a massive overhaul of their trading infrastructure, not only focusing on drastically lowering latency levels within the single bank platforms, but also on developing a more efficient pricing engine and internalization capabilities to better manage their risk books against different types of customer segments. It was also during this time that the banks decided to kick out those high frequency trading firms whose relationships they deemed unprofitable.

Since 2008, however, banks and certain segments of the high frequency trading community are attempting to peacefully co-exist. As banks continue to increase their internalization efforts, potential liquidity from high frequency trading firms has become more attractive. On the other hand, high frequency trading firms have come to realize that banks have a vital position in the FX market; in order to ensure continued success, co-opetition has become a competitive necessity.

One potential change that could change the balance in the market is successful implementations of centralized clearing in the OTC marketplace. If non-bank high frequency trading firms can become direct clearing members for OTC products, and also illustrate their commitment to taking more risk as a legitimate liquidity provider, banks' stranglehold in the FX market could be weakened and hence open up a new phase of intense competition.

Projected Presence of High Frequency Trading in FX

The presence of high frequency trading flow in FX has been increasing every year, even through the rough-and-tumble 2008–2009 time frame. Its presence can be felt in many different ways. Similar to the cash equities market, one good indicator is the total number of daily trades. In 2001, the global FX market averaged slightly more than 200,000 trades daily.

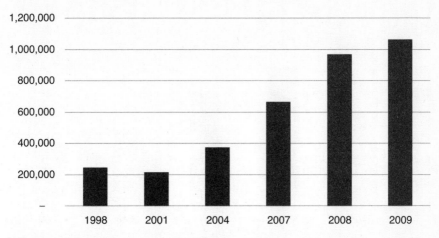

FIGURE 6.9 Increasing Number of Trades Per Day
Source: BIS, Bank of England Foreign Exchange Joint Standing Committee (JSC), New York Foreign Exchange Committee, Singapore Foreign Exchange Market Committee, Canadian Foreign Exchange Committee, Tokyo Foreign Exchange Joint Standing Committee, ECNs, and Aite Group

At the end of 2009, the average daily trade figure reached more than 1 million trades a day. Figure 6.9 displays the estimated average of trades per day.

Another good indicator of high frequency trading's impact in the marketplace is the overall trend in average trade size. In addition to the explosive growth in average daily trade number, the FX market has also seen a decline in average trade size. In 2005, the average trade size for spot FX stood at close to US$4 million. By the end of 2009, the average trade size had shrunk to US$1.4 million. Figure 6.10 shows the declining average trade size in spot FX.

FX high frequency trading is poised to grow quite rapidly over the next few years, as the first-generation high frequency trading firms are joined by an influx of next-generation equity and futures high frequency trading firms looking to capture uncorrelated alpha in FX. In addition, new high frequency trading firms have emerged in recent months, formed by FX quants and traders who have left large banks looking to capture new opportunities on the other side of the market. At the end of 2009, high frequency trading accounted for approximately 25% of overall trade volume. This figure is expected to hit more than 40% by the end of 2012. Figure 6.11 shows the estimated market share of HFT in the FX market.

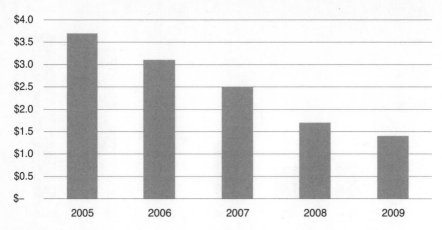

FIGURE 6.10 Declining Average Trade Size in Spot FX (in US$ Millions)
Source: Aite Group

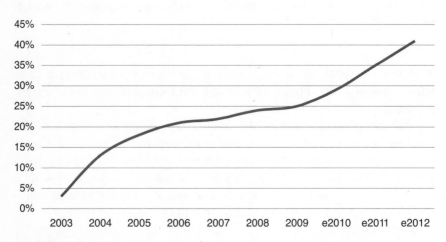

FIGURE 6.11 Estimated Market Share of High Frequency Trading in FX
Source: Aite Group

EQUITY OPTIONS

The equity options market has always been described as a quote-driven market. The quotes generated are from the designated market makers that each exchange employs. The market makers are required to make a two sided market for a certain amount of time per day. Each exchange has their own rule book which they update on a regular basis. The current

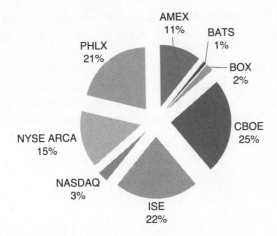

FIGURE 6.12 Equity Options 2010 Market Share
Source: Options Clearing Corp

landscape has a total of eight active exchanges. They are BATS, Boston Options Exchange (BOX), American Stock Exchange (AMEX), NYSE ARCA, Chicago Board of Options Exchange (CBOE), NASDAQOMX, Philadelphia Exchange (PHLX), and the International Securities Exchange (ISE). The 2010 market share is shown in Figure 6.12.

The battle for market share between the exchanges is one that continues on a daily basis. When it comes to high frequency trading certain exchanges implemented the same model as the equity exchanges had done. The model called, maker/taker, is based on traders earning rebates for providing liquidity. This model has been adapted but not without traditional customer discontent. The traditional exchanges namely the CBOE and the ISE have always given priority to customers when it came to top of the order book. So defining who is a customer and who is a legitimate market maker has always been a point of disagreement within the industry.

High frequency trading in equity options has increased due to exchange competition (pricing models) and penny pricing. Since there are so many names (symbols) and expirations the only way to provide liquidity is through HFT technology. Traders in equity options need to be separated into different buckets of classifications. The first bucket is the designated market makers who stream prices on multiple symbols on multiple venues. Without the lowest latency and most stable network, an equity option market maker will get run over and be out of the business rather quickly. Some of the market makers also internalize retail flow from the many online equity options brokers. This retail flow allows for market makers to make money as they are much less price sensitive than an institutional player. The second bucket of HFTs is looking to earn rebates in the maker taker exchanges (NYSE ARCA, BATS, BOX, and NASDAQOMX), and they also provide a two-way market, within markets, in less volatile times. When the market gets active they will more likely take liquidity than provide it. As always each HFT has different strategies and defining them the same way is not fair.

OVER THE COUNTER DERIVATIVES

Regulatory changes in the U.S. will change the way standardized derivative products trade. For years only voice brokers executed business. The products will now be required to trade electronically. The most commonly traded product is the interest rate swap. Other swaps such as the credit default swap, currency swaps, and various commodity swaps are also actively traded. The high frequency trading community is always willing to trade products that are liquid and have trading data available. Now with an electronic market being mandated they will have the chance to participate for the first time.The swap markets have always been controlled by the large broker dealers who have little interest in letting other players enter this area of trading. Although there are many details to be ironed out by the regulators, the OTC markets have the potential to be a area of future growth for HFT.

EXPANSION INTO GLOBAL MARKETS

High frequency trading is no longer an U.S. equities market phenomenon. In addition to expansion into other asset classes, high frequency trading firms have aggressively branched into other markets.

European Market

Since the explosive growth of alternative execution venues in the United States, the European exchanges have been bracing for similar competition over the last decade. Similar to the experience in the U.S. market, the fundamental trigger of market structure change has been a landmark pan-European regulation named the Markets in Financial Instruments Directive

(MiFID). MiFID is by far the most ambitious piece of regulatory initiative within the European financial services industry. At the highest level, MiFID is designed to achieve the following goals:

- Provide pan-European harmonization in order to promote investor protection and the leveling of competition across borders.
- Improve market transparency.
- Create an environment for greater market competition for trade execution.
- Create a pan-European mandate to uphold best execution obligation.

Of course, as with most things in life, noble goals often do not automatically generate desirable results. In the U.S. equities market, the Order Handling Rule of 1997—a set of rules originally designed to dissuade questionable limit-order handling practices of NASDAQ market makers—resulted in massive market fragmentation and competition with the rise of ECNs.

The question for the European market is: Will regulatory efforts to improve the overall market transparency and pan-European competition lead to unintended consequences of market fragmentation and less market transparency that will ultimately benefit only a handful of large global banks at the expense of the general public?

Some of the important elements of MiFID, which will have a direct impact on the evolution of the pan-European market structure, include:

- *Best execution burden.* Firms are required to formulate, maintain, and demonstrate their best execution policies and practices on behalf of their clients. They will be required to maintain a five-year history of customers' trades, own quotes, and trade execution data, as well as statistics on execution venues used to complete execution, etc. The ability to capture, store, and analyze accurate and timely trade and customer-related data will be key to successful regulatory compliance. This key element of MiFID compliance will put additional pressure on the data management infrastructure of all key European market participants.
- *Bypassing concentration rules.* In certain European countries, under the Investment Services Directive (ISD) of 1993, all orders had to be sent to regulated exchanges for execution. MiFID will enable firms to bypass any existing concentration rules within specific domestic markets, which will lead to increased competition amongst the market execution venues. Related to this, off-exchange executed trade

information (i.e., internalized trades, upstairs trading, ATSs [alternative trading systems], etc.) can be reported to other venues that are outside of the traditional exchanges. Other venues can include multilateral trading facilities (MTFs), market data consolidators, and more. Sensing an opportunity to create a pan-European trade capture and market data distribution platform, an industry consortium named Project Boat was created by leading brokers/dealers.

- *Mandate for firm public quotes and transparency requirements.* In the interest of enhancing pre-trade price discovery, MiFID will mandate that those firms that are active internalizers publish firm public quotes. Also known as systematic internalizers (SI), these firms will be required to publish their quotes and trade execution data concerning those securities traded on regulated markets on a regular and continuous basis to meet pre- and post-trade disclosure mandates.

Taken together, these key MiFID elements point to various new market opportunities and pitfalls. One market opportunity has certainly been identified by various global brokers/dealers already—increased market share in trade execution.

Over the last two and a half years, multiple venues have emerged from the dust of MiFID, including MTFs and dark pools. These alternative venues are expected to account for more than 30% of pan-European equities trade volume by end of 2010. Figure 6.13 shows an estimate of the breakdown of the European market share.

With faster systems and infrastructure, these new destinations have led to a proliferation of technology-savvy, latency-sensitive high frequency traders. By the end of 2010, high frequency trading is expected to account for over 30% of all trading in the European equities market. Figure 6.14 displays a projection of the European equities market.

As these new types of clients materialize and traditional clients become more sophisticated at varying rates, brokers have had to amend and adapt their offerings to suit the individual and unique needs of their diverse client traders. Brokers have expanded their traditional, simple benchmark strategies into strategies that incorporate dynamic, real-time variables, customization, and low latency infrastructure.

Asian Market

The Asian markets are at a crossroads. Driven by initiatives from the global broker/dealer community and operators of alternative execution

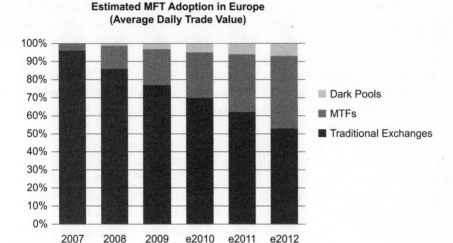

FIGURE 6.13 European Market Share
Source: Exchanges, MTFs, Brokers/dealers, Aite Group

venues, basic business and IT infrastructures for increased market competition are being developed. Expected competition across different liquidity pools and adoption of sophisticated liquidity management tools have generated much excitement and doubts within the major Asian financial centers.

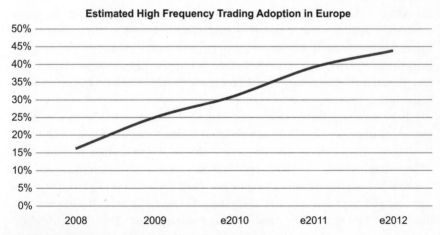

FIGURE 6.14 Projected European Equities Market
Source: Aite Group

Not surprisingly, uncertainty and resistance still exist within the various domestic players looking to hold onto their entrenched competitive positions. Throughout Asia, there are regulatory, IT, business, and cultural obstacles that may hamper the overall adoption of impending market structure changes. However, if the experiences of the U.S. and European markets are any indication, dramatic market structure changes appear inevitable and those firms that are able to embrace these changes first should have a significant competitive advantage in the long-run.

Unlike the U.S. and European markets, there is no single pan-Asian capital market. Each major Asian financial center has its own set of regulations and infrastructure, which makes it very tough for smaller players to build a significant presence in Asia. However, despite certain regulatory, infrastructural, and cultural obstacles, market structure changes are occurring across major Asian financial centers, evidenced most recently by the launch of Arrowhead in Japan.

Regulatory Disparity   The biggest hurdle for market innovation has been the lack of a Pan-Asian market concept. This has also led to the absence of a centralized pan-Asian regulatory body and harmonized market standards, which have forced firms to take a country-by-country approach, prolonging the overall adoption cycle. Each country has its own set of issues and concerns, and market practices are dictated by local customs and beliefs.

In general, most Asian markets discourage off-exchange transactions. Certain regulations, such as the one in Australia, make it very difficult for ATSs and financial institutions to engage in non-displayed crossing. Australia's lead market regulator, Australian Securities Investments and Commissions (ASIC), has been preoccupied with a financial system that is plagued with its own difficulties due to the global economic crisis. This has placed the consideration of ATSs, such as AXE ECN, on the regulatory back burner until recently.

In Hong Kong, Singapore, and Japan, crossing of listed securities is allowed for offshore clients. South Korea remains strict in its approach to allowing alternative execution venues outside of the exchange. The glimmer of hope comes from Instinet, which has partnered with Samsung Securities to provide the nation's first crossing network, called KoreaCross. The platform gained approval in early 2008 from Korea's Ministry of Finance and the KRX, albeit with heavy-handed help from Samsung Securities, Korea's largest investment bank. In Korea, ATSs without onshore business presence must partner with a local broker to have access to the local market.

Based on regulatory status and changes in market structure and ex-change technology upgrades, Japan appears to be the most ready for first-generation ATS adoption. This potential has been boosted by the recent launch of Arrowhead, the Tokyo Stock Exchange's (TSE's) next genera-tion trading and market data platform. Unlike other Asian markets, Japan's proprietary trading system (PTS) activity has increased over the last few months.

Overall, major regulatory changes must be made and uniform stan-dards must be adopted within most Asian financial centers to initiate in-creased market competition and adoption of sophisticated trading tools.

Need for Local Customer Education and Change in Local Struc-ture   While the prospect for cheaper executions is certainly appetizing, local buy-side customers are not thrilled about the potential trade-off for increased complexity in market structure and additional spending in their own IT infrastructure to compete.

While most domestic and foreign brokers have adopted advanced trad-ing technologies, the local buy-side community still relies heavily on tele-phones and brokers to meet their trading objectives. Lack of IT knowledge on the buy-side adds complexity to driving the adoption of advanced trade execution tools, which includes direct market access (DMA), algorithms, and ATSs. Successful adoption of ATSs requires adoption of advanced trading applications such as Order Management System and Execution Management System platforms as well as the implementation of smart-order routing technologies on the part of the brokers and third-party vendors.

Depending on the country, clearing and settlement is another area of concern. In Hong Kong, Australia, and Singapore, the primary exchanges own the clearing and settlement organizations. ATSs view clearing and set-tlement falling under the umbrella of the incumbent exchanges as a conflict of interest. This is primarily because even if and when ATSs get market approval, the clearing and settlement agencies really have no incentive to work with them in an efficient and timely manner so that they can become fully operational as soon as possible. This presents another hurdle for ATSs to overcome and further delays competition in the Asia-Pacific region.

Emergence of Alternative Execution Venues   Hampered by the lack of pan-Asian regulations and robust trading infrastructure, adoption of ATSs in Asia is expected to lag behind both U.S. and European markets for many years. Still, throughout Asia, a number of promising ATSs have

TABLE 6.1 List of Alternative Execution Venues in Asia

Firm	Launch Date	Country of Operations	Ownership	Type
AXE ECN	N/A	Expected in Australia, New Zealand	NZX, Citigroup, CommSec, Goldman Sachs, JBWere, Macquarie Bank, and Merrill Lynch	Displayed
BlocSec	2008	Hong Kong, Singapore, Japan	CLSA Asia-Pacific Markets	Non-Displayed
Chi-East	2010	Singapore	SGX and Chi-X	Non-Displayed
Chi-X	2010	Expected in Australia, Japan	Nomura Holdings Inc.	Displayed
Kabu.comPTS	2006	Japan	Kabu.com, Credit Suisse, Mitsubishi UFJ Securities, UBS, BNP Paribas, and Nikko Citi	Displayed
Liquidnet Asia	2007	Hong Kong, Singapore, Japan, Australia	Liquidnet Holdings	Non-Displayed
Monex Nighter	2001	Japan	Monex	Displayed
SBI Japannext	2007	Japan	SBI Holdings, Goldman Sachs, Rakuten, ORIX, CLICK, Credit Suisse, Merrill Lynch, and Lehman Brothers	Displayed

emerged over the last few years in anticipation of major market structural changes. Table 6.1 lists the alternative execution venues in Asia.

- *Japan.* Some of the earliest ventures into the alternative liquidity markets can be traced back to Japan. However, the first-generation ATSs (referred to as PTSs in Japan to denote their legal name as proprietary trading systems) originated typically from retail online brokerage firms looking to add trade volume during after market hours. However, in recent years, SBI Japannext and Kabu.comPTS have attracted investments from global brokers and have launched competitive services during TSE market hours.

- *Australia.* After years of regulatory limbo, there are signs of movement in the Australian market, which the likes of AXE ECN, Chi-X, and Liquidnet have been waiting on to open up. With the approved handover of market supervision from the Australian Stock Exchange (ASX) to the Australian Securities Investments and Commissions (ASIC), legal foundation is now in place for new exchanges to enter the market, with Chi-X expected to be leading the charge.
- *Singapore.* BlocSec is a crossing network for institutional investors looking to execute block trades of securities listed on the SGX (Singapore Exchange). The expected launch of Chi-East, a non-displayed pool joint venture between SGX and Chi-X is being watched quite closely as it is the only example in Asia where an incumbent exchange is working closely with a potential rival to create an alternative pool.

In addition to these alternative pools, brokers have also launched their non-displayed crossing engines across key financial centers in Asia. Sample brokers and their crossing capabilities across a few major Asian financial centers are highlighted in Table 6.2.

While independent ATSs struggle to begin operations faced with inflexible regulations, most brokers/dealers have operated their own internal crossing platforms for a couple of years now, mainly focused on the Japanese and Hong Kong markets. As the markets become more electronic and major Asian market centers begin to fragment, these internal crossing engines will enable brokers/dealers to provide a wide array of liquidity services to their clients.

Adoption of Direct Market Access and Algorithms   Despite the fact that the development of the ATS market is lagging behind, brokers/dealers continue to build up their arsenal of DMA and algorithms for their Asian clients. Most global firms that have brought most of their suite of algorithms from the U.S. and European markets have created local quant groups to customize the algorithms to meet the needs of the various Asian markets.

TABLE 6.2 Sample List of Crossing Platforms in Asia

Broker	Crossing Platform	Australia	Hong Kong	Japan	Korea	Singapore
Credit Suisse	Crossfinder	■	■	■	■	■
Goldman Sachs	SIGMA X	□	■	■	□	□
Instinet	CBX in HK and Japan, JapanCross in Japan, KoreaCross in Korea	□	■	■	■	□
ITG	POSIT	■	■	■	□	□
Merrill Lynch	MLXN	□	■	■	□	□
Morgan Stanley	MS Pool	□	■	■	□	□
Tora Trading	Clearpool and Crosspoint	□	■	■	□	□
UBS	PIN	■	■	■	□	□

Projected Adoption of High Frequency Trading   The overall adoption of high frequency trading in Asia is expected to lag behind Europe by a significant margin driven by the lack of IT infrastructure, complexity in regulation, and lack of attractive market microstructure. However, the presence of high frequency trading firms in most of the major Asian markets confirms that given the right mixture of conditions, the penetration of high frequency trading flow could be significant and quite rapid. Figure 6.15 shows a projection of HFT in Asia-Pacific.

South America

The latest entrant in the automated trading craze is located in South America. The Brazilian market has changed drastically in the past few years, with the BM&F and Bovespa merging alongside the elimination of an open-outcry trading floor. As recently as the 1990s, more than 20 different markets existed in Brazil. Over time, they have consolidated into one equity market: Bovespa. Trading of various types of securities is still very much separated, however, while Bovespa has been electronic for some time, the BM&F futures market has only been electronic since July 2009.

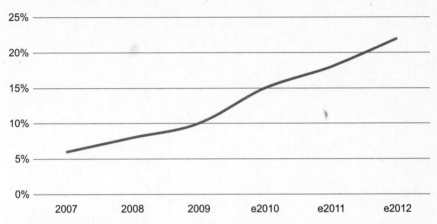

FIGURE 6.15 Estimated Adoption of High Frequency Trading in Asia-Pacific
Source: Aite Group

The Brazilian derivative market is denominated by listed futures and options. Investors are trading interest rate, currency, equity index, and commodity futures. The main interest rate contract is the one-day term interbank deposit contract. The active currency pair contract is the U.S. dollar versus the Brazilian real. Each currency contract is worth US$50,000. The Commodity Futures Trading Commission's (CFTC's) Office of General Counsel announced that it issued a no-action letter on August 26, 2009, permitting the offer and sale in the United States of full-sized and mini-sized futures contracts based on the Ibovespa Index. The miniature contract is identical to the large contract except that it is one-tenth the amount of the large contract.

CHAPTER 7

Positives and Possibilities

A ite Group estimates that trading firms spent more than US\$1.3 billion on electronic trading infrastructures in 2010. The challenge of executing trades across multiple liquidity points in milliseconds is easy to discuss and difficult to implement. It takes innovation, and that innovation drives new technology into the market at large. Consider some of the technological innovations driven from low latency trading demands:

- *Complex event processing.* This technology gained commercial prominence through algorithmic trading. Now, telecommunications companies use it for switch routing and banks use it for fraud detection. That one component of a low latency trading infrastructure represented a more than US\$40 million technology investment last year, and is headed into the mainstream in the next generation architecture discussions.
- *High-performance messaging middleware.* Aite Group estimates that capital markets firms spent about US\$220 million on messaging middleware associated with electronic trading in 2010. While firms like TIBCO and IBM capture the majority of this market, disruptive technologies by upstarts have carved out a niche, forcing latent large players to start innovating again.
- *Hardware acceleration.* Right now, capital market firms are investing in the next generation of hardware platforms. Technology companies are creating new methods for writing software directly to processing

cards and bypassing input/output (I/O) limitations to achieve microsecond response times. Imagine the potential benefits to other sectors.

- *In-memory databases.* Data caches stored in-memory allow technologists to keep aggregated views of highly transactional data current so data that used to be stored in an information silo can be joined with more latent data, enabling firms to make much faster decisions based on real-time continuous queries.
- *Solid-state drives.* The solid-state drives in our Netbooks are small these days. As another shortcut around I/O latency bottlenecks, capital market firms are demanding bigger drives. Ultimately, those larger-capacity drives will end up in the laptops and Netbooks we carry, creating faster, lighter, and more stable machines.
- *Unstructured data processing.* Electronic trading firms are exploring new ways of processing semantic information like news feeds, Twitter feeds, social networking content, and other unstructured data for seeking opportunities and mitigating risk. Imagine the potential applicability to other sectors, which will be able to monitor counterparties and identify risk in real-time.

These are just some of the innovations paid for by the electronic trading race. Defense, intelligence, telecommunications, manufacturing, and many other sectors benefit from these technological advances without having to fund all of the associated research and development.

Leading the innovation curve is expensive. Right now, high frequency trading (HFT) belongs to a very small group of firms globally. The technical barrier to entry is high and it takes capital to fund a strategy. Expect that to change. Trading firms living on speed today may find the race getting more crowded and more competitive in the very near future. Speed will soon become a commodity available to almost anyone with an appetite for high volume trading.

COMMODITIZING HIGH FREQUENCY TRADING

While HFT firms continue to gain share in markets that can digest their trading activity, mid-market brokers/dealers, quantitative strategy managers, hedge funds, and traditional asset managers are all forced to play keep-up in order to acquire adequate fills for their own portfolios. While these other market participants may not need sub-millisecond latency to support their trading activity, they certainly need single-digit millisecond response times in order to be "in the game." Because of this, managed trading platforms are gaining ground for firms that do not consider low-latency trading infrastructures competitive differentiators in their business. Further, sponsored access continues to drive business for managed trading solution providers among high frequency firms, particularly in risk management.

The commercial landscape is rich with options. It appears that while many of the leading traditional execution management solution (EMS) providers have hit their commercial apex and are now on the market, new low-latency trading solutions are cropping up on a regular basis. Market options vary from point solutions to fill in gaps from internal development all the way to managed "HFT-in-a-box" solutions encompassing a full suite of trading technology. A complete managed trading solution includes the following:

- *Platform.* All of the hardware required for usage in a managed environment.
- *Colocation.* Rack space at the colocated facilities of the relevant matching engines.
- *Network connectivity.* All of the fiber between instances of the platform. For instance, high-speed fiber between Chicago and New York or New York and London.
- *Market data.* All of the feed handlers, ticker plant, and connectivity to direct feeds. Some even include historical data access for back-testing and blended strategies with executions based on historical indicators.
- *Order management.* Some combination of order management (not all solutions are for black box trading), direct execution management, or smart order routing (SOR) capabilities.
- *Risk management.* Perform pre-trade risk checks to protect both the trading firm and their sponsor.
- *Algo chassis.* Platform to host custom algorithms (algos). In some cases, providers include basic algo packages with their platform.
- *Compliance reporting.* Provide reports for the sponsoring broker across their customer base.
- *Latency monitoring.* Tools to assess latency, self-heal line connection issues, and tune to optimal performance.

In order of importance, market data ranks at the top for solution priorities (see Figure 7.1). The trading network and access to global markets rank second and third respectively.

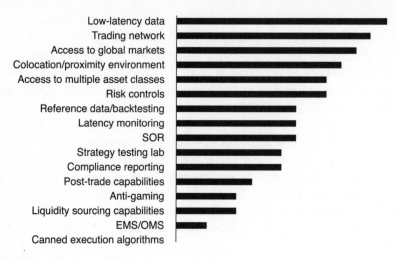

FIGURE 7.1 Key Components to a Managed Trading Solution
Source: Aite Group interviews with 48 electronic trading firms

Few vendors support all of the required functionality internally. That does not seem to matter to a majority of people. We found that 60% of respondents indicated they preferred a collection of best-of-breed solutions to a consolidated solution. So, vendor partnerships may be a key attribute to a successful solution. The current diversity is a positive attribute of the community. Vendors vary widely in origin, capability, and geography. Small start-ups, broker/dealer funded solutions, exchange-provided technology, and even proprietary technology supplied by other high frequency firms dot the commercial landscape.

TRADING TECHNOLOGY DEMANDS AND PREFERENCES

The most important facet to trading a new asset class or geography is figuring out whether one can actually make money at it. To do that, many firms look for technology that allows them to execute a proof-of-concept prior to setting up multi-year contracts with colocation facilities, telecommunications providers, and other essentials that lock firms into a long-term commitment. Firms also struggle finding development resources to build

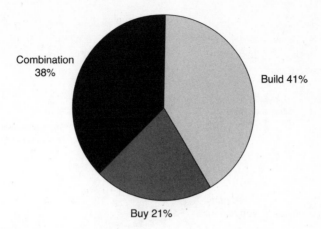

FIGURE 7.2 Build or Buy Preferences
Source: Aite Group interviews with 48 electronic trading firms

competitive technology in new markets. While the perception exists that most HFT firms prefer to build everything in-house, that perception is not true. In fact, most would prefer to either buy their technology outright or buy some of the plumbing and build what they consider their competitive differentiators (see Figure 7.2).

Still, half of all technology is built in-house (see Figure 7.3). Vendors comprise another 27% of the stack. Brokers are only supplying nine percent of the technology stack.

INTERNAL FOCUS

Internal development efforts parallel vendor efforts in most areas. Thirty firms told us their top three development priorities for the next year. The common themes include:

- *Colocation.* Key requirements included colocation for new markets and asset classes, data center consolidation, and moving additional strategies into existing colocation. Further, firms were waiting for new colocation opportunities to come online from exchanges and other liquidity providers.
- *Market data.* Key requirements include acquiring more direct feeds, new data to support expansion, and building historical data repositories for back-testing strategies.

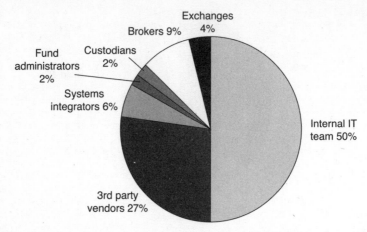

FIGURE 7.3   Key Technology Providers for Low-Latency Trading
Source: Aite Group interviews with 48 electronic trading firms

- *Risk management.* Speed is the key requirement for risk management. How fast can trades make it through required checks and can the firm make it faster? Further, many firms are watching regulatory discussions and preparing to incorporate additional risk management requirements.
- *Geographic and asset class expansion.* This is a large bucket largely containing the other items in this list, but additional efforts primarily focus on making internal changes to existing systems to support new data types, new fields, new connectivity methods, and is probably the largest bucket of outsourcing opportunity and interest.
- *Network connectivity.* Key requirements in this area include upgrades to routers, the addition of network monitoring tools, and fiber upgrades.
- *General Latency.* Key requirements include hardware upgrades, exploring hardware acceleration, engineering code for multi-core, and squeezing latency out of existing code.

CHOOSING VENDORS

In our discussions with many of these firms, it would be fair to say that perceptions about the capabilities of the vendor community are outdated. Some conversations discussed evaluations of vendors that no longer

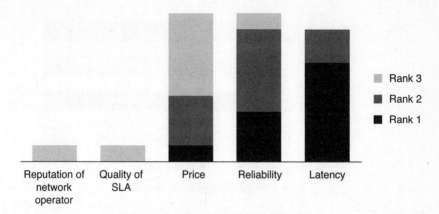

FIGURE 7.4 Key Criteria for Network Vendor Selection
Source: Aite Group interviews with 48 electronic trading firms

existed or were acquired by other solutions. Other conversations talked about the last evaluation times, which were up to two years ago. Two years is a lifetime in low latency trading technology. The reason this is important becomes obvious when examining what firms look for in providers. In the case of providers that also supply the network infrastructure, latency is by far the top selection requirement (see Figure 7.4).

Reliability follows latency, with price after that. In fact, we did not find the HFT community particularly price sensitive. Sure, there was a lot of complaining about price in our discussions, but nobody said they chose the runner-up because that vendor was cheaper. In terms of the technology stack required for sponsored access, the same order held true, only with latency becoming an even more critical component (see Figure 7.5)

The good news for firms looking for technology is that the vendor community offers quite a few options. Further, with a combination of vendor saturation and technology improvements like hardware acceleration, finding affordable solutions that offer low latency and reliability gets easier every day.

FINDING THE NEXT OPPORTUNITY

High performance databases (HPDBs) play a central role in quantitative trading. From data acquisition through production, a full-featured HPDB is the data warehouse, data mining application, complex event processing

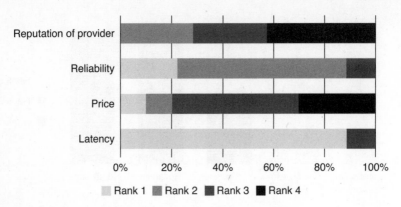

FIGURE 7.5 Key Criteria for Sponsored Access Technology
Source: Aite Group interviews with 48 electronic trading firms

(CEP) engine, and live-scenario test harness all rolled into one package (see Figure 7.6).

In a typical high performance trading infrastructure, the HPDB manages two architectural layers:

- The HPDB is the functional repository for time-series market data. Unlike a standard database, which reads rows of data, HPDBs are column-store databases. When looking for a particular value, the HPDB does not scan each row for record matches. It is more like dropping a bucket down a well for water than like strip-mining the ground, layer after layer, until water is reached. The former is much faster than the latter.

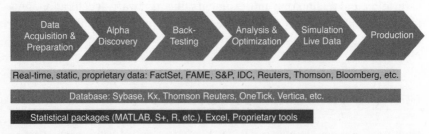

FIGURE 7.6 Partial Quant Analysis Infrastructure Ecosystem
Source: Aite Group

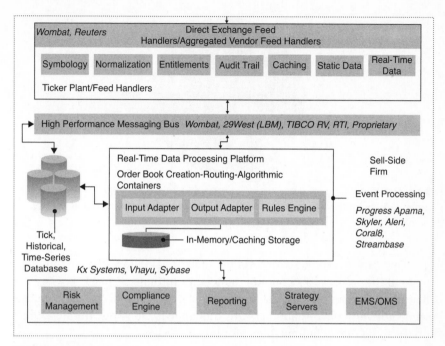

FIGURE 7.7 High Performance Trading Infrastructure
Source: Aite Group

- The HPDB typically serves as the in-memory location for data used for active analysis and/or to run real-time trading. In Figure 7.7 both functions are represented by blue database icons.

While those two areas comprise the current functionality of the average HPDB, a third is making its way into the mix: Complex event processing (CEP). OneMarketData, Sybase, and to some degree, Kx, support internal CEP engines for both data playback and signal generation. All vendors that do not currently support CEP, have partnerships with leading CEP providers.

Regardless of where the lines start and end, HPDBs will play an important role in the march across asset classes and geographies as quants look to chart a course into new territory.

Speed is essential for firms running strategies that feature both real-time and historical data. Aite Group estimates that 90% of quantitative trading firms currently maintain or are developing at least one trading strategy that requires playing back historical data in conjunction with real-time data (see Figure 7.8).

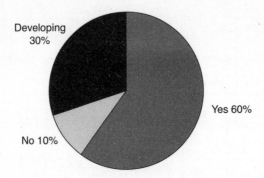

FIGURE 7.8 Strategies Running Real-Time and Historical Data
Source: Aite Group (estimates based on discussions with a dozen quant firms)

One firm we spoke with leveraged historical data with real-time data to time the impact of economic indicators hitting the market. They run historical simulations against scenarios like ten-year swaps performance while non-farm payroll numbers are announced, and adjust trading signals on the fly as that economic indicator hits the market.

Nearly every firm we spoke with stores raw market data. A few firms derive bars for data over a certain age, but all recent data was full-depth for every trading venue for every firm interviewed. Most strategies require a certain amount of raw data to be effective. Even the most esoteric trading strategies require a certain amount of raw data. One firm we spoke with performed statistical analyses on economists. They time economic data versus economic releases to calculate which economists know what they're talking about and how they affect the market.

Very few firms we interviewed think historical data had much value prior to decimalization, though one firm said they found value in older historical data for FX (foreign exchange) strategies. Most strategies looked at data that was between two days and six months old. Given the volatility in the market, many strategies consider data more than a few months old irrelevant, or, in one case, impossible to run on existing hardware before the firm runs out of processing power.

ISSUES AND RISKS

Regardless of the value of storing years of data to trading strategies, regulatory requirements mandate that firms have to store more tick data. The

Markets in Financial Instruments Directive (MiFID) in Europe and Regulation National Market System (Reg NMS) in the United States both mandate reporting capabilities for proving best execution. Many HPDBs serve the dual purpose of quantitative analysis and housing best execution information in order to feed these reporting engines. Aite Group expects firms to have even more onerous reporting requirements as regulatory oversight continues to increase in the current political environment. The Securities and Exchange Commission (SEC) says it plans to renew efforts to look at market manipulation and insider trading. Most new initiatives come with new reporting requirements.

As they add instrument classes, geographies, and even new data types, storage is becoming an issue. Some firms are now storing petabytes of information. From a monetary perspective, it would make sense to store data in a shared cloud and run back-testing off the cloud. Despite this, quantitative traders fear being gamed by other cloud participants watching them run their strategies. Storage also has an impact on data volume increases—increasing data volumes adversely affect HPDBs as much, if not more, on the data writing-process as it does on the data-reading process.

Another significant risk for HPDBs is basic business agility. One firm we spoke with, which had built its own HPDB, was concerned that its internal solution would not be able to handle the firm's expansion into equities. While adding new data types will be the norm in 2010, many firms will find they have been boxed out of new market opportunities by technology selection.

Data volumes also affect firms' ability to perform complex calculations fast enough to have an impact on the market. One firm stopped using its HPDB for real-time signal generation because it was not fast enough for their trading frequency. Most firms we spoke with leveraged multiple libraries for calculations, including MATLAB, S+, and R. One firm built its own proprietary calculation language into its HPDB, and was able to achieve a calculation improvement of a factor somewhere between 10 and 30 times over out-of-box libraries.

ORDER ROUTING GETS SMART

While the focus of market impact and fairness by media and the U.S. Congress seems to be on the high frequency trading firms, they only represent one percent of the SOR market (see Figure 7.9).

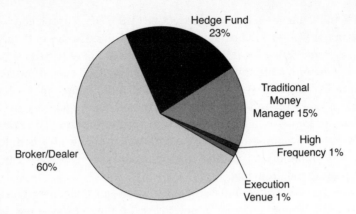

FIGURE 7.9 Who Uses a Smart Order Router?
Source: Vendor survey responses

While these firms invest heavily in technology, many either trade on a single venue to maximize speed or tend to build their technology internally as a perceived competitive advantage. Instead, brokers/dealers (including banks) represent 60% of the SOR market. Hedge funds outnumber traditional asset managers for the remainder of the market. Lastly, execution venues support a small share of the market, including hosting arrangements with other third-party providers in their data centers as a value-added service.

That market segment could change. With many liquidity venues aggregating in data centers or having third-party proximity hosting options, there are more possibilities for high frequency trading across multiple asset classes. Further, there are fiber connections between Chicago and New York in the low double-digit millisecond range. With cross-asset and cross-geography ultra-low latency trading becoming more possible every day, high frequency firms will need smarter order routing to capitalize on market structure innovation.

Payment for access to smart order routing can vary. Some charge per execution, some charge license and maintenance, and some involve soft-dollar arrangements as part of a bundled service. Regardless of format, Aite Group estimates that SOR clients globally are paying US$772 million for access to SOR technology (see Figure 7.10).

Further, Aite Group expects demand to increase over the next 12 months, in part supported by guerilla marketing through the attention on high frequency trading, till it exceeds US$1 billion in 2010.

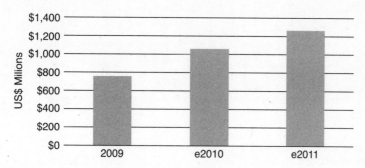

FIGURE 7.10 Spending for SOR Technology
Source: Aite Group estimates

The majority of those dollars support brokerage providers. Aite Group expects 95% of the firms leveraging a smart order router do so through one or more brokerage providers (see Figure 7.11). Trading technology providers—which comprise a mix of execution management systems providers, hybrid trading platforms, and trading networks focused on specialized executions—are supported by another four percent of that business. Lastly, complex event-processing providers have captured another one percent of the market.

Aite Group sees little shift between the three groups in the near future. Challenges associated with building and maintaining smart order routers will keep them from becoming a staple on the average firm's build list (see Figure 7.12).

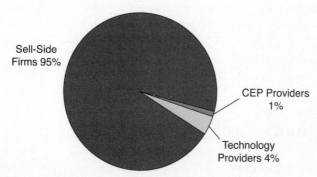

FIGURE 7.11 SOR Market Share by Provider Type
Source: Aite Group estimates

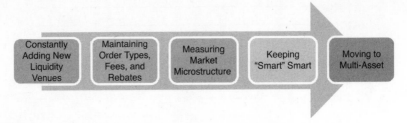

FIGURE 7.12 Challenges with Smart Order Routing
Source: Aite Group

The most obvious challenge is the ever-expanding pool of liquidity sources. Staying connected to order books is a perpetual process, and most of the suppliers profiled in this report list additional connectivity in their top development priorities.

Beyond liquidity venues, keeping up with order types, rebates, market data feed modifications, and other incremental changes initiated by individual liquidity venues adds a maintenance headache for SOR suppliers.

Assuming a firm can connect to an expanding list of venues and maintain the changes associated with each venue, measuring the market within a market—the microstructure—becomes the next daunting challenge. Competitive smart order routers need to know exchange latency, advantages to specific order types, liquidity refresh rates for specific instruments on specific venues, fill rates on specific dark pools, and a myriad of other nuances that must be measured and back-tested.

Once the microstructure gets accumulated and analyzed, those nuances need to be turned into the logic that determines the most efficient routing for a given order. Further, users need to be able to apply a sliding scale between price improvement and speed (passive versus aggressive) to each order and have that logic adjust to customer input.

Once the SOR is connected and tuned so it runs like a Ferrari, the business will inevitably come back with a request to trade a new asset class or move into a new market. At that point, the process starts all over again.

SMART ORDER ROUTING'S FUTURE

The first rule of retail is said to be location. The same can be said for the next-generation smart order routers. Only one-third of the participating providers currently offer colocated or proximity-located services, though

Aite Group expects that to grow as more opportunities arise for space in data centers.

Product diversification is also a critical component of the next generation of SORs. Not only will SORs need to service multiple product lines simultaneously; they will also need to perform sophisticated arbitrage between the products. For instance, in trading an ETF (exchange traded fund) based on the S&P 500 (Standard and Poor's 500 index), the SOR will need to price each underlying security to determine whether to buy and sell individual securities or the ETF. Similar functionality will be required for options.

More sophisticated microstructure measurement will also be common in next-generation smart order routers. Firms like Corvil, Correlix, and others provide latency monitoring tools for low latency trading infrastructures. These vendors have started performing point-to-point latency monitoring from exchange data centers. Aite Group expects that level of detail to play a role in routing tables at some point in the near future.

Next, expect the SOR world to begin receiving and digesting more data. We asked sixteen firms as part of this research if they were planning to incorporate some kind of ancillary data like economic indicators or news into their order routing in the next year. More than 60% of them indicated they either had plans or were evaluating the possibility (see Figure 7.13).

Lastly, expect better reporting. We heard this demand from customers more than any other. Existing reports can be as simple as a spreadsheet that gets manually updated each day. Customers expect at some point in

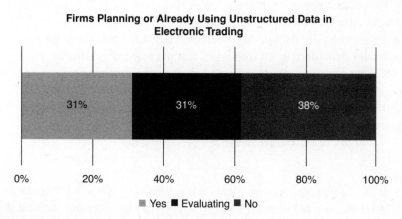

Firms Planning or Already Using Unstructured Data in Electronic Trading

31%   31%   38%

0%   20%   40%   60%   80%   100%

■ Yes   ■ Evaluating   ■ No

FIGURE 7.13 Moving Beyond Market Data
Source: Interviews with 16 firms doing electronic trading

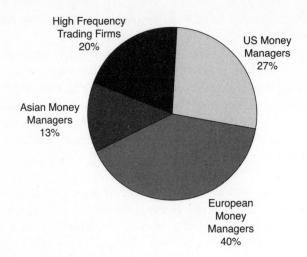

FIGURE 7.14 Where Is SOR Growth Potential?
Source: Vendor pipelines, Aite Group estimates

the future to be able to calculate trade cost on-the-fly, see detailed transaction cost analysis (TCA) reporting, and satisfy Reg NMS and MiFID best execution reporting requirements through their SOR provider. Some even expect to be able to see and tune client commissions.

Market fragmentation and global trading are driving SOR adoption. Of the areas driving growth, Europe is leading the interest in adoption (see Figure 7.14).

European money managers are responding to MiFID requirements with SOR implementations, both to prove best execution and keep up with the expanding pool of liquidity choices. They have proven to be an eager market for providers. High frequency trading firms have also been exploring SOR providers. Asian money managers are just starting to look at SOR. As the Japanese market fragments and other Asian countries follow U.S. and European market structures, Aite Group expects Asia to experience significant growth.

A number of business drivers are propelling SOR growth:

- *Dark Liquidity Access.* Firms with standard execution capabilities need more sophisticated tools to access hidden liquidity without displaying their intention to the market. Further, keeping up with new liquidity venues and their associated attributes is a challenge.

- *Liquidity Access in a New Geography.* There are a number of reasons firms might be looking beyond their local markets, including arbitrage opportunities and general interest in emerging markets.
- *Customized Trading Algorithms.* Firms are looking for more control over their trading strategies. Customers are pushing providers to supply more parameters, wider thresholds, and custom strategies for clients looking to perform more sophisticated execution strategies.
- *Small-Firm SOR Adoption.* Buy-side managers with less than US$100 million assets under management are attractive to several of the participating providers because this segment is just starting to adopt more sophisticated trading technology and lacks the resources to build and maintain it internally.
- *New Asset Classes.* The fastest-growing market for smart order routing among the trading firms we spoke with is in the FX market for currency arbitrage. Options are another strong area for firms interested in moving beyond equities.
- *Compliance.* Compliance with best execution requirements is a major driver for European firms, which makes reporting capabilities at providers a key piece of functionality.

IS ARTIFICIAL INTELLIGENCE NEXT?

Unstructured data is information not generally read or interpreted by computers to make decisions. There is normally an associated context beyond a number that requires some perspective to interpret. In the trading world, market data is structured information that drives trading. News, Internet content, and Securities and Exchange Commission filings have been components of an unstructured data universe that are now receiving structure and/or context to be leveraged in algorithmic trading. Aite Group expects firms to begin incorporating new sets of unstructured data into their trading strategies to either enhance or circumvent electronic trading's technology race.

ECONOMIC INDICATORS

While not entirely unstructured, economic indicators have been the early adopters' content of choice for electronic trading strategies. They are particularly important for the trading of Foreign Exchange products. Now that more people in trading understand indicators' effects on the market, they are becoming more popular as ancillary trading information. Economic indicators are released by governments to report on the health of a sovereign economy. In the United States, the key indicators include the Consumer Confidence Index, Gross Domestic Product, Jobless Claims Report, and others.

Economic indicators as they relate to electronic trading are also increasingly dependent on technology for providing a competitive edge. Government agencies like the Department of Labor and Department of Commerce have strict rules for reporting economic indicators: If a particular indicator is supposed to be announced at 8:30 A.M. on a Friday morning, the media will be allowed to enter a lock-up environment at 7:30 A.M., in which they may have no communication with the outside world. They are allowed to see the release and ask questions of the representatives in lock-up, and they may prepare the release prior to announcement, along with any context they may wish to provide associated with the questions they are allowed to ask. Once the lock-up period is over, reporters can connect their computers to the Internet and transmit the data. At that point, receipt and processing of the indicator are dependent on the network speed between the source and the customer's trading system. Like market data dependencies, economic indicators as used in electronic trading involving sub-second demands.

Demand for low-latency reporting of economic indicators has been increasing in the last year and suppliers are being asked to expand their geographic coverage. Risk management needs are also driving demand for economic indicators, which are used to loosen and tighten spreads, halt trading, or hedge a position with FX. While other unstructured data offers more diversity in trading, Aite Group expects economic indicators to continue fueling the drive beyond market data for electronic trading.

NEWS

Commercial news has been a staple in capital markets from the dawn of trading, and the strength of firms like Dow Jones, Bloomberg, Reuters, and others testifies to the significance of news in trading. Further, news has expanded to 24-hour television with CNBC and the relatively new Fox Business channels. Beyond the staples of corporate information tracking, there is a myriad of specialty publications that require tracking depending on the breadth and depth of a particular company. Their industry, product, social activism, research and development, and in some cases the personalities of the leadership team, may all be tracked in unique publications. Each news source has to be taken in context and measured according to the applicability to the company and the semantic information associated with the news item.

Once all of the sources are in place, firms can then start to look for patterns among the news and how they correlate with market conditions. Taking it one step further, firms can then assign weightings to news based on whether or not a story indicates positive, neutral, or negative news about a company. This is called semantics.

Applying semantic weightings to news items requires a substantial amount of up-front work associated with understanding language. To a reader, a company's earnings report reported as *good* and *not good* mean different things. A computer needs to be taught that *not good* also means *bad*. Using slang, *bad* can also mean *good*. *Exploding* can be about a bomb or about growth. If you are having difficulty following the change, imagine how hard it is for a computer to determine the context of each word. Language nuance makes it difficult to teach computers how to decide an execution strategy (or halt one) based on the context of an article. Further, news semantics for trading does not evaluate an article. Instead, semantic evaluation requires the program to evaluate the company or companies in the article and evaluate their context in the story.

SECURITIES AND EXCHANGE COMMISSION FILINGS

In April 2005, the Securities and Exchange Commission announced an initiative to move financial reporting to an electronic filing system. In the electronic filing process, data is published using eXtensible Business Reporting Language (XBRL) to segregate financial information into structured eXtensible Markup Language (XML) documents that can be read by XBRL document readers and machines. Adoption in the United States has been slow, but some pilot fund companies and a few public entities have begun offering XBRL reporting. Microsoft was the first to step up to the task (Figure 7.15).

Japan has been an enthusiastic adopter of XBRL. After two small pilot programs in 2007, Japan began requiring companies to submit annual reports, semi-annual reports, quarterly reports, and registrations via XBRL starting in April of 2008. The goal of XBRL is to open financial reporting up

```
<msft:BusinessSegmentsOutlookTextBlock contextRef="FY08Q3_ST">For the fourth
quarter of fiscal year 2008, we expect continued growth in both product and
services revenue. We expect product revenue growth from platform adoption
through new and renewal volume licensing growth coupled with our new product
offerings.</msft:BusinessSegmentsOutlookTextBlock>
- <!- Revenue ->
<us-gaap:SegmentReportingInformationRevenue contextRef="FY08Q3_ST_Gaap"
decimals="-6" unitRef="USD">3255000000
</us-gaap:SegmentReportingInformationRevenue>
<us-gaap:SegmentReportingInformationRevenue contextRef="FY07Q3_ST_Gaap"
decimals="-6" unitRef="USD">2748000000
</us-gaap:SegmentReportingInformationRevenue>
<msft:OperatingRevenue_OneYearDelta_Div_OperatingRevenue
contextRef="FY08Q3_ST_Gaap" decimals="2" unitRef="Pure">0.18
</msft:OperatingRevenue_OneYearDelta_Div_OperatingRevenue>
<us-gaap:SegmentReportingInformationRevenue contextRef="FY08YTD_ST_Gaap"
decimals="-6" unitRef="USD">9433000000
</us-gaap:SegmentReportingInformationRevenue>
<us-gaap:SegmentReportingInformationRevenue contextRef="FY07YTD_ST_Gaap"
decimals="-6" unitRef="USD">8087000000
</us-gaap:SegmentReportingInformationRevenue>
<msft:OperatingRevenue_OneYearDelta_Div_OperatingRevenue
contextRef="FY08YTD_ST_Gaap" decimals="2" unitRef="Pure">0.17
</msft:OperatingRevenue_OneYearDelta_Div_OperatingRevenue>
- <!- Operating Income ->
<us-gaap:SegmentReportingInformationOperatingIncomeLoss
contextRef="FY08Q3_ST_Gaap" decimals="-6" unitRef="USD">1092000000
</us-gaap:SegmentReportingInformationOperatingIncomeLoss>
<us-gaap:SegmentReportingInformationOperatingIncomeLoss
contextRef="FY07Q3_ST_Gaap" decimals="-6" unitRef="USD">911000000
</us-gaap:SegmentReportingInformationOperatingIncomeLoss>
<msft:OperatingProfit_OneYearDelta_Div_OperatingProfit
contextRef="FY08Q3_ST_Gaap" decimals="2"
unitRef="Pure">0.20</msft:OperatingProfit_OneYearDelta_Div_OperatingProfit>
<us-gaap:SegmentReportingInformationOperatingIncomeLoss
contextRef="FY08YTD_ST_Gaap" decimals="-6" unitRef="USD">3220000000
</us-gaap:SegmentReportingInformationOperatingIncomeLoss>
<us-gaap:SegmentReportingInformationOperatingIncomeLoss
contextRef="FY07YTD_ST_Gaap" decimals="-6" unitRef="USD">2656000000
</us-gaap:SegmentReportingInformationOperatingIncomeLoss>
<msft:OperatingProfit_OneYearDelta_Div_OperatingProfiTt
contextRef="FY08YTD_ST_Gaap" decimals="2"
unitRef="Pure">0.21</msft:OperatingProfit_OneYearDelta_Div_OperatingProfit>
```

FIGURE 7.15 XBRL Example: Microsoft Q3 2008
source: Microsoft Investor Relations Web site

to investors and researchers to find interesting details on a real-time basis and be able to compare those details against historical performance, projected earnings, other companies in the sector, and other useful research. In fact, one of the popular use cases these days involves parsing out executive compensation information. For algorithmic trading, XBRL can be leveraged to bypass news related to financial reporting and get the numbers in a machine-readable format at the same time the reporter receives them, without having to wait for the write-up.

While XBRL holds promise for applying unstructured data to trading, Aite Group does not expect abbreviated worldwide adoption; the regulatory bodies involved in pushing the XBRL initiative are a little busy with other priorities these days.

THE PSEUDO-SEMANTIC WEB

Arguably no content source involved in electronic trading today is less structured than the Internet. Of content sources mentioned in this report, none is also more open to interpretation as a "trusted source" than the Internet.

The Internet is also big. Google engineers announced through their blog that they had indexed over one trillion unique URLs as of July 2008. Tracking relevant information can be more daunting than finding that proverbial needle in a haystack. As the Internet continues evolving with Web 2.0 technologies (blogs, wikis, Really Simple Syndication (RSS) feeds, etc.), the number of contributors to available content has also expanded. People with something to say now have technology to support their voice without needing special software or an understanding of HyperText Markup Language (HTML). Research analysts use tools today that create agents to track specific content relevant to their coverage area.

Companies like Connotate and JackBe allow web researchers to create search agents and build mashups of relevant content into a single page. For instance, someone tracking General Electric (GE) may want to monitor consumer sites for new product ratings feedback, job sites for GE job postings, and various blog sites by GE employees. Figure 7.16 represents an aggregated number from multiple job posting sites collected daily by a Connotate Agent.

However, aggregating that relevant information and tracking it against its ability to predict the market are still very people-oriented processes. Further, there is no back-testing data available for building these scenarios.

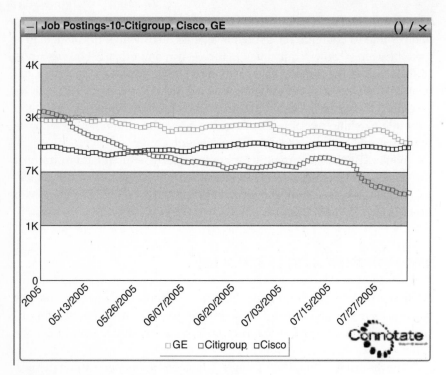

FIGURE 7.16 Connotate Job Posting Tracking
Source: Connotate

That data needs to be accumulated internally. So, if someone has the idea to track a technology company's product sales potential against books sold related to that technology, they have to accumulate a significant period's worth of data to adequately test their theory.

Further, website content aggregators are currently built for human consumption. The aggregators are designed to compile information on a periodic basis and display the compiled results through a portal. There would need to be some work involved to turn an aggregator into a machine-friendly provider. Users would also have to balance aggregation latency with courtesy. A research analyst may need the data aggregated once a day at most. A news algorithm may need far more update iterations. However, people who clog Web sites with requests that slow those Web sites down can be blocked from access through their Internet Protocol (IP) addresses. The malicious version of this behavior performs this exponentially more frequently and is referred to as a denial of service attack. A company like Amazon.com is not going to like a full scan of their top toy sales occurring every second during the holiday season by a Web agent program. That activity could slow their website down and hurt sales.

While news services provide machine-readable content to electronic trading firms, people involved in advancing the World Wide Web have been working on a framework for transforming the Internet into both human and machine-readable content. Referred to as the "Semantic Web" or Web 3.0, the idea is very similar to how news services attach metadata to stories for machines to more easily parse and understand unstructured content.

Unlike XBRL, there is no uniform taxonomy associated with the advancement of the Semantic Web. Standard XML can be used to add context to different sections of a Web page, but some proponents of Semantic Web technology support a Resource Description Framework (RDF). The framework was developed as a metadata model to augment HTML and essentially tags subsets of content to identify specific attributes of web content for parsing by computers.

HTML is the underlying framework for how a Web page is laid out. For instance, **semantic** is HTML for *semantic*, though without any context. Adding *<rdf:Description>* implies the word *semantic* describes something that would be referenced in a subsequent tag. The problem with augmenting HTML with RDF is that it doubles the work of creating a Web site. In addition to creating the content, an author now has to think about the context of each word in that content and how that word might apply to the overall context of the content. The process is similar to a Customer Relationship Management (CRM) or document management solution that makes the user assign content types to every piece of information in a document instead of just saving the document.

Because of the difficulty Internet contributors face with applying metadata to online content, it will take many years to migrate relevant content on the Internet into its own semantic ontology. However, trading firms need not wait for Web 3.0 to segment content for trading purposes because it is possible to generate repeatable results that machines can understand using HTML patterns on a website.

One of the current challenges with using online sources in electronic trading is trust. Is that Web site delivering accurate information? Is the blog written by a former employee with "disgruntled" preceding his or her status? Is that union Web site reporting credible information about ending the strike? There are a host of credibility questions that need to be asked by people pointing algorithms toward Internet content. Discussions among people interested in unstructured content about regulating news feeds as trusted or untrusted sources exists due to the United Airlines occurrence, but the SEC can hardly regulate the Internet.

GOING GLOBAL

With four primary news services focused on providing low-latency news for electronic trading purposes, news becomes another horse race akin to market data. In the world of economic indicators, that aspect is already becoming reality, at least for key United States indicators. Among content providers for economic indicators, there is a significant push to offer indicators for more markets. However, those that tire of keeping up with the technical requirements associated with low-latency trading may decide to think outside the box: The information that holds the greatest competitive advantage may not be available to capital markets today. Thomson Reuters indicated they have customers asking for metadata tags in Kanji news for tracking the Japanese market and those global companies doing business in Japan. Adding those tags may offer a step toward tracking a global market: Why stop at one country?

Imagine being able to track news from a multitude of countries depending on where the companies being traded operate. As Dubai continues to grow as a major market center, imagine being able to track Middle-Eastern newspapers or even closed-caption feeds from Al Jazeera for news about oil as a commodities trader in a machine-readable format. As China continues to grow as a prime emerging market, imagine being able to track local news about particular factories, environmental issues, or other information that may offer a competitive edge for a trading firm covering a company based thousands of miles away. Imagine being able to compile information on weather, disease, politics, and other information at a macro level.

One of the pieces of information tracked as part of a semantics package involves how unique a piece of information is relative to the other news being published on a particular company. As the list of trusted sources—or semi-trusted sources, depending on the freedom of the press—grows, the ability to gain unique perspective grows. While major news tends to find its way out of a market and into mainstream press, there is inherent latency in that process. Further, not all information makes it into the mainstream. Something not deemed particularly relevant to the world at large may be extremely relevant to a trading firm and one of the instruments it tracks. In that case, the winners and losers of the electronic trading world are not the haves and have-nots of the fastest hardware colocated next to the exchange of choice.

Tracking news on a global basis is not easy or cheap. If it were, more capital market firms would already be doing it. First, a firm needs to hire a specialist for each foreign language. That specialist is responsible for helping determine appropriate news sources and developing the metadata associated with each source. The specialist needs to develop the semantic structure of the language, monitoring and adjusting slang and local dialect to improve accuracy. Someone in a non–English speaking country, for example, would need to know that the U.S. reaction, "That new product is sick!" should not trigger a short-selling algorithm of the company based on the adverse health of the new product. Patience is also a required virtue. Many of these news sources may not provide a rich archive to test trading scenarios, like the news archives offered by the vendors profiled in this report. Instead, trading strategies need to be monitored for some time in order to build confidence in the firm's model.

THE NEXT WAVE

Thanks to global interest and outsourcing, we are exporting capital markets domain expertise at the same time we are importing technology skills. What barrier is there in today's electronic market for someone to combine the two for their own benefit on a global basis? Think about it. As the technology becomes more accessible for testing strategies and deploying them in a managed environment, low latency trading could become available to anyone anywhere. In places like India, Russia, and other strong math centers, we could see a wave of trading.

Colocation is available. There are managed trading platforms and sponsored access. It would seem that anyone with technical acumen, an understanding of the markets, and some statistical analysis skill could build a strategy and start trading in a low latency environment. Sure, capital is a barrier to entry, but there are firms out there willing to fund people with a good strategy. People in the Ukraine, India, the Philippines, Malaysia, etc. will figure out how to turn their technical acumen and market knowledge into a profitable strategy.

CHAPTER 8

Credit Crisis of 2008

The Blame Game

T he financial crisis of 2008 was a perfect storm, with much finger-pointing toward responsible parties. While no one contributor was solely responsible, all participants—the U.S. Federal Reserve (Fed), regulatory agencies, credit agencies, politicians, and the end-users and institutions that brokered such deals—need to reflect and make changes to decrease the likelihood of another economic collapse.

U.S. FEDERAL RESERVE

The Fed's monetary policy over the last 20 years has never been described as tight. The Goldilocks economy pursued by the Fed in the mid- to late-1990s tried to produce consistent growth with little inflation. This, of course is a logical goal, but the reality is the hardest decision a central bank needs to make is to raise interest rates in the anticipation of an economic crisis or a market bubble.

The New York Federal Reserve's bailout of Long Term Capital in 1998 set a terrible precedent, creating a mind-set that any fund or a firm deemed by the market as "too big too fail" would be backed by the Fed, despite any bad loans or investments. This mentality inspired additional risk-taking by hedge funds and Wall Street firms. Counterparty risk—which should be to investors the number one priority—was perceived as less of an issue, so long as the investor and the trading partner fell into the systemic risk category.

REGULATORY AGENCIES

Underfunded and fragmented, regulatory agencies failed in their role of protecting investors, especially in the case of Bernie Madoff. Provided with information that Madoff was allegedly front-running or perpetrating fraud, the Securities and Exchange Commission (SEC) failed to uncover the fraud during their investigation. Aite Group believes all regulatory agencies need to employ a staff that understands the diverse amount of products that are available. The other problem is the regulatory gap that exists when it comes to the over-the-counter (OTC) marketplace.

Credit products have received the most press, but massive amounts of other OTC products such as interest rate swaps, currency swaps, and commodity swaps are outstanding.

CREDIT AGENCIES

Credit agencies are responsible for evaluating public firms and providing a rating for their creditworthiness. This function is extremely important to the marketplace, as any firm that suffers a negative ratings change will see its financing costs increase. The agencies are paid by the issuer of the securities being reviewed. This conflict of interest has always been an issue, but there was little outcry for change prior to the credit crisis. The agencies decided to rate complex products when securitization became popular. The staff at the agencies made many assumptions about credit risk as the historical data available could not effectively reflect the risks of a potential meltdown in credit. The institutions involved in this market needed an investment grade rating of these products to hold them. The false sense of security that an investment-grade rating provides is no excuse for investors not to do their own due diligence.

POLITICIANS

The pay-to-play system that has been plaguing our political environment for many years is at the forefront of this crisis. Donors and lobbyists constantly jockey for position for the yearly government spending that is available at taxpayers' expense. When it comes to the financial markets, the lack of knowledge of our representatives and senators is astounding. The committees that will recommend regulatory changes are not up to date on the technology changes the markets have experienced, and thus remain at the mercy of the many influence peddlers that control Washington. Producing legislation on a bipartisan basis is extremely important for gaining credibility and reassuring the market that the new regulatory environment will not be changed in two or four years.

END-USERS OF DERIVATIVE PRODUCTS

The mismanagement of derivative products is nothing new. The Orange County, California debacle of 1994 is a perfect example of an end-user who gets in over their head. The county had to file for bankruptcy due to losses from investments in certain derivative products made by the treasurer. The risk back then was interest rates related, as the Federal Reserve increased base rates unexpectedly, and the owners of swap-related derivatives never accounted for a major move in the yield curve. That situation turned out not to be systemic, but the lesson should have been learned: The buyers and sellers of such products each need to understand the risks involved with their investments. Investors underestimating the risk of a major counterparty going bankrupt and the aggressive use of leverage are the ultimate reasons for the current situation. Credit derivatives were created to provide a hedging tool for investors of corporate bonds. The participants in the marketplace, specifically the sellers of protection, became complacent, collecting premiums with no concern for a potential default. Investors who use derivatives employ different pricing models. A typical model will use a certain number of variables that yield a theoretical price that is used in judging whether the derivative is fairly priced by the market or is overvalued or undervalued. One of the most well known models is the Gaussian copula. The model used historical market data instead of historical default data to price credit derivatives, specifically, collateralized debt obligations (CDOs), which in theory, simplified the risks of the products by producing a single correlation of the likelihood of all of its mortgages in the CDO defaulting on their debt at once. The actual model was not the problem, but the universal acceptance of the model by the trading community was. The combination of investment managers looking for additional yield, and investment banks salespeople looking for large year-end bonuses created a free for-all. When investors—in this case CDOs and credit default swaps (CDSs)—are all piling into the same trade, a pyramid investment bubble begins to build, with no end in sight. The market became vulnerable to an once-in-a-lifetime credit event that no model predicted. The marketplace may never be the same.

RECENT REGULATORY HISTORY

The regulatory gaps that exist today came from changes in the regulatory structure implemented in the last decade. Both the Financial Modernization Act of 1999 and Commodity Futures Modernization Act of 2000 were originally billed as modernizing prior statutes. What they really did was begin the deregulation era.

FINANCIAL MODERNIZATION ACT OF 1999

Also known as the Gramm-Leach-Bliley Act (GLBA), the Financial Modernization Act of 1999 repealed provisions of the Glass-Steagall Act of 1933, which restricted the ability of bank-holding companies to affiliate with securities firms and insurance companies. GLBA substantially modernized the U.S. financial services industry, but made only incremental changes to financial services regulation. As a result, U.S. financial conglomerates could operate in virtually all areas of financial services, but the regulatory structure remained largely institutional. The act split up the oversight of conglomerates among government agencies: The Securities and Exchange Commission would oversee the brokerage arm of a company, bank regulators would supervise its banking operation, and state insurance commissioners would examine the insurance business, but no single agency would have authority over the entire company.

COMMODITY FUTURES MODERNIZATION ACT OF 2000

When the Commodity Futures Modernization Act of 2000 was signed into law back in December of 2000, the goal was to clarify two issues:

- To allow trading of single stock futures with the oversight being shared by the CFTC (commodity futures trading commission) and the SEC. This part of the act provided an opportunity for both regulatory bodies to work together to set and enforce rules. Although single stock futures are very popular in Europe, the market in the United States has not taken off.
- The act clarified that certain OTC derivatives were outside the jurisdiction of the CFTC. The act also exempted energy trading on electronic platforms from regulation. This part of the act became known as the "Enron loophole," as OTC energy swap contracts now became unregulated. In the absence of proper regulation, traders were able to amass large positions in the energy market without any position limits. Many market participants believe that this legislation was responsible for the surge in energy prices over the last decade.

DODD FRANK WALL STREET REFORM ACT OF 2010

The credit crisis of 2008 has led to another legislative attempt to re-shape the regulatory landscape. Filling in the regulatory gaps that existed in the OTC markets is one of the many areas that were addressed. While overall the bill does address many of the issues, the complexity and length of the new bill is causing uncertainty in the business community. The legislators did miss out on a golden opportunity to consolidate the existing regulatory agencies. The SEC and the CFTC will have a joint effort in regulating OTC products with all swap products now falling under their scrutiny. The most notable changes are listed below.

The Consumer Financial Protection Bureau

- *Independent Head:* Led by an independent director appointed by the President and confirmed by the Senate.
- *Independent Budget:* Dedicated budget paid by the Federal Reserve System.
- *Independent Rule Writing:* Able to autonomously write rules for consumer protections governing all financial institutions—banks and non-banks—offering consumer financial services or products.
- *Examination and Enforcement:* Authority to examine and enforce regulations for banks and credit unions with assets of over $10 billion

and all mortgage-related businesses (lenders, servicers, mortgage brokers, and foreclosure scam operators), payday lenders, and student lenders, as well as other non-bank financial companies that are large, such as debt collectors and consumer reporting agencies. Banks and Credit Unions with assets of $10 billion or less will be examined for consumer complaints by the appropriate regulator.

The Financial Stability Oversight Council

- *Expert Members:* Made up of ten federal financial regulators and an independent member and five nonvoting members, the Financial Stability Oversight Council will be charged with identifying and responding to emerging risks throughout the financial system. The Council will be chaired by the Treasury Secretary and include the Federal Reserve Board, SEC, CFTC, OCC, FDIC, FHFA, NCUA, and the new Consumer Financial Protection Bureau. The five nonvoting members include OFR, FIO, and state banking, insurance, and securities regulators.
- *Tough to Get Too Big:* Makes recommendations to the Federal Reserve for increasingly strict rules for capital, leverage, liquidity, risk management, and other requirements as companies grow in size and complexity, with significant requirements on companies that pose risks to the financial system.

ENDING TOO BIG TO FAIL BAILOUTS

Limiting Large, Complex Financial Companies and Preventing Future Bailouts

No Taxpayer Funded Bailouts: Clearly states taxpayers will not be on the hook to save a failing financial company or to cover the cost of its liquidation.

Discourage Excessive Growth & Complexity: The Financial Stability Oversight Council will monitor systemic risk and make recommendations to the Federal Reserve for increasingly strict rules for capital, leverage, liquidity, risk management, and other requirements as companies grow in size and complexity, with significant requirements on companies that pose risks to the financial system.

Volcker Rule: Requires that regulators implement regulations for banks, their affiliates, and holding companies, to prohibit proprietary trading, investment in and sponsorship of hedge funds and private equity funds, and to limit relationships with hedge funds and private equity funds. Nonbank financial institutions supervised by the Fed will also have restrictions on proprietary trading and hedge fund and private equity investments. The Council will study and make recommendations on implementations to aid regulators.

CREATING TRANSPARENCY AND ACCOUNTABILITY FOR DERIVATIVES

Bringing Transparency and Accountability to the Derivatives Market

- *Closes Regulatory Gaps:* Provides the SEC and CFTC with the authority to regulate over-the-counter derivatives so that irresponsible practices and excessive risk-taking can no longer escape regulatory oversight.
- *Central Clearing and Exchange Trading:* Requires central clearing and exchange trading for derivatives that can be cleared and provides a role for both regulators and clearinghouses to determine which contracts should be cleared. Requires the SEC and the CFTC to pre-approve contracts before clearing houses can clear them.
- *Market Transparency:* Requires data collection and publication through clearing houses or swap repositories to improve market transparency and provide regulators with important tools for monitoring and responding to risks.

HEDGE FUNDS

Raising Standards and Regulating Hedge Funds

- *Fills Regulatory Gaps:* Ends the "shadow" financial system by requiring hedge funds and private equity advisors to register with the SEC as investment advisers and provide information about their trades and portfolios that are necessary to assess systemic risk. This data will be shared with the systemic risk regulator and the SEC will report to Congress annually on how it uses this data to protect investors and market integrity.

- *Greater State Supervision:* Raises the assets threshold for federal regulation of investment advisers from $30 million to $100 million, a move expected to significantly increase the number of advisors under state supervision. States have proven to be strong regulators in this area and subjecting more entities to state supervision will allow the SEC to focus its resources on newly registered hedge funds.

CREDIT RATING AGENCIES

New Requirements and Oversight of Credit Rating Agencies

- *New Office, New Focus at SEC:* Creates an Office of Credit Ratings at the SEC with expertise and its own compliance staff and the authority to fine agencies. The SEC is required to examine Nationally Recognized Statistical Ratings Organizations at least once a year and make key findings public.

EXECUTIVE COMPENSATION AND CORPORATE GOVERNANCE

Give Shareholders a Say on Pay and Creating Greater Accountability

- *Vote on Executive Pay and Golden Parachutes:* Gives shareholders a say on pay with the right to a nonbinding vote on executive pay and golden parachutes. This gives shareholders a powerful opportunity to hold accountable executives of the companies they own, and a chance to disapprove where they see the kind of misguided incentive schemes that threatened individual companies and in turn the broader economy.

The new legislation gives new demands to a regulatory structure that has an inconsistent track record. When it comes to high frequency trading (HFT) the SEC and CFTC are actively reviewing the components of the business.

IMPACT OF POTENTIAL REGULATIONS AND RULE CHANGES—SECURITIES AND EXCHANGE COMMISSION CONCEPT RELEASE

The SEC started a broad review of the market structure of the U.S. equity market back in January of 2010. The goal was to do an assessment on whether market structure rules have kept pace with changes in trading technology. The agency has a long-standing duty to uphold the interest of the long-term investor. The idea of being a buy-and-hold investor is now in doubt as anyone who started investing in the year 2000 can understand. The buy-and-hold strategy is really more of a myth concocted by the mutual fund industry so they can continue to earn management fees. There is always a time to buy and sell a stock and the time horizon can truly be long term. The target remains the short-term trader and high frequency trading is the poster child.

According to the SEC Concept Release, the SEC considers all HFT firms to be recognized as proprietary trading firms who may or may not be registered as a broker/dealer, and also may reside within a multi-service broker-dealer or operate as a hedge fund. The major characteristics of HFT firms are their use of extraordinary high-speed and sophisticated computers for generating and executing orders. In addition they use colocation services and individual data feeds offered by exchanges. HFT firms have a very short time-frame for establishing and liquidating positions and the submission of numerous orders that are cancelled after submission and ending the trading day in as close to a flat position as possible. So the good news is that the agency does have a reasonably solid understanding of the trading style.

The other areas of interest to the SEC include quality of liquidity, liquidity rebates, order anticipation strategies, momentum strategies, and fairness of colocation.

CHAPTER 9

Conclusion

The high frequency trader story is one of how the shift of power in a profitable business can create a firestorm of misunderstanding. As all the listed markets went electronic the process of buying and selling securities changed forever. There is no longer a human being creating the prices for others to trade upon. Some have made the transition to the new electronic marketplace and others have not. Those whose livelihood have changed dramatically and are negatively impacted by the change are the ones most likely to complain. Is the new market perfect? Far from it, but there will always been an inherit risk to investing. The idea that the stock market over the long haul will have guaranteed profits is a fallacy created by the industry itself. After serious research the regulators created a competitive marketplace in the equity market and they should stand by their decisions. Competition has lead to tighter spreads and cost of trading has decreased significantly. This is fact and just because the power has shifted to the high frequency liquidity providers does not mean there is a smoking gun of manipulation and fraud.

The majority of problems during the great recession were caused on the credit side where there are many suspects to blame. The listed markets actually performed extremely well during the crisis and in its aftermath. Of course naysayers will bring up May 6th, 2010 and this is a legitimate reaction to a day that will not be remembered in a positive way. Blaming automated traders for that day is again just another misinformed reaction by the investing public. Trading is risky and always will be when markets are going higher; no one seems to care about automated trading then. When there is a negative fundamental shift in a market, a correction will indeed happen and in some cases the price action will be scary. This does not mean there cannot be positive changes in market structure. Events like May 6th, 2010 will lead to changes that hopefully will be well thought out and with the understanding that there may be unintended consequences.

For the high frequency trading community there will be continued expansion in other asset classes as well as global expansion. The trend towards electronic trading will continue and with the addition of certain over the counter products going electronic, the area where high frequency traders will trade will also increase. The controversy surrounding the subject will continue as the idea of machines taking over the world will always exist. You will never trust what you cannot see.

Glossary

A

Agency Dark Pool Operated typically by independent agency brokers, agency dark pools attempt to cross various client orders that flow through the broker without principle interest in the trade.

ATS Alternative trading system, execution service provided to buy-side institutions.

Automated Trading Execution of a trade strategy without human intervention.

B

Block Trading Dark Pools Seek to provide a trading environment in which large orders can be crossed with minimum market impact.

C

CEP Engine Complex Event Process, technology for low-latency filtering, correlating, aggregating, and computing on real world event data.

Circuit Breakers Procedure to stop the trading of a security or index at a certain percentage for the previous day's closing price.

Colocation The physical location of an actual trading model at or near data centers hosting exchange matching engines.

Commercial Hedgers Firms who use the futures market to hedge their interest rate, currency, or commodity risk.

Consortium Dark Pool Broker/dealer owned dark pool.

Co-opetition A hybrid competitive reality in which market participants both, compete and cooperate with one another for market share.

Counterparty   Firm who takes the opposite side of a transaction.

D

Dark Pool   Execution venues that do not provide public quotes.

Decimalization   The process of changing the prices that securities trade from fractions to decimals.

Depth of Book   Buy and sell prices that are below or above best buy or sell price.

Direct Market Access   Process of allowing a trader to send their orders directly to the exchange matching engine.

E

ECN   An electronic communication network created to compete with the existing equity exchanges.

Exchange Dark Pool   A dark pool owned and operated by an exchange.

F

Feed Handlers   Technology that compiles exchange market data feeds.

Filtered Sponsored Access   Allows the sponsored participant to gain direct access to market centers via a dedicated port provided by the sponsoring broker.

Flash Order   An order type that allows a trader to see if there is any interest to buy or sell at a certain price point prior to the order being sent to other venues.

Floor trader   Trader whose physical location is on an exchange trading floor.

H

High Frequency Trading   Electronic trading strategy that is characterized by holding time of position.

Holding Time   The amount of time a buyer or seller of a security keeps its position.

HPDB   High performance database, column stored database that is used by HFTs.

I

Indication of Interest (IOI)   Non-binding interest in buying or selling a security.

Institutional Trader   Trader whose risk is inherited by his or her company.

Internalization Dark Pool   The largest of the dark pool category, internalization dark pools encompass those broker-operated dark pools that can utilize their own account to execute against client order flow.

L

Latency   Measure of a time delay of an order reaching an exchange matching engine.

Limit Order Handling Rule   This rule mandates that market makers receiving limit orders inside their spread must handle these orders in one of three ways. Incorporate the price into their quote in NASDAQ quote montage, execute the limit order immediately, or send the order to another market participant.

Liquidity   Amount of what is available to buy or sell of a security or commodity at a particular price.

Liquidity Mapping   Provides real time statistical predictions in terms of routing options among the various dark pools.

M

Market Maker   Firm or individual who provides a bid (buy price) and offer (sell price) for others to trade upon.

Matching Engine   An exchange software engine that matches up buyers and sellers.

Messaging Middleware   Software that provides an interface between applications, allowing them to send data back and forth.

MIFID   Markets in Financial Instruments Directive, European regulatory directive similar to Reg NMS (see ahead) that requires firms to prove best execution of their client's orders.

MPID   Market participant identification, an exchange provided trading identifier.

O

OTC   Over-the-counter, trade execution that is not completed on a listed exchange.

OPRA   Options Price Reporting Authority, authority that reports the amount of market messages generated.

P

Prop Shop   Firm that trades for its own account and does not handle customer funds.

Q

Quantitative Trader   Trader who employs mathematical relationships in their trading strategies.

Quote Display Rule   This rule bans market makers from posting one quote in the NASDAQ quote montage and a different quote for the same stock in an alternative trading network.

R

Rebate   An exchange payment to a trader who provides liquidity.

Reg NMS   Regulation National Market System, a Securities and Exchange Commission regulation designed to uniformly set rules across all U.S. equities market centers to improve market transparency and to guarantee fair access for individual investors.

S

Scalper   Trader who takes small profits or losses many times per day.

Smart Order Routing   Process of sending an order to buy or sell at the best price as well as to which venue offers the lowest cost to execute.

SOES   Small order execution system, created after the crash of 1987 to handle automatic execution capabilities on a price-time priority.

Speculator   Firm or individual who takes a position in a market without any real use for the security or commodity.

Sponsored Access   A non-member entity (i.e., a sponsored participant) gaining direct access to market centers by using the MPID of a member broker/dealer (i.e., sponsoring brokers), leveraging access infrastructure not owned by the sponsoring broker.

Storage   The process of archiving historical trading data.

Stub Quotes   Bid/offer quote that is away from the current market price to meet a market maker obligation.

T

Ticker Plant   Technology that takes data from financial exchanges, processes it, and delivers it to traders' desktops.

Top of Book   Best buy and sell price for a security that trades electronically.

Trade Reporting Facility   Electronically facilitates the post-execution steps of price and volume reporting, comparison and clearing of trades for NASDAQ-listed securities, as well as for transactions in NYSE- and other U.S. regional exchange-listed securities that occur off the floor.

Trading Algorithm   Model-based program that determines what action to implement next as market data updates.

U

Unfiltered Sponsored Access   Also known as "naked" access. Under this sponsored model, the sponsored participant gains direct access to the market centers via a dedicated port provided by the sponsoring broker, but lacks real-time pre-trade risk monitoring by the sponsoring broker.

About the Authors

PAUL ZUBULAKE

Paul Zubulake is a senior analyst at Aite Group, LLC, specializing in financial, energy and commodities futures, and options markets. His expertise includes how the application of technology, such as algorithmic trading and Financial Information Exchange (FIX) protocol, is playing an ever-increasing role in futures and options trading.

Mr. Zubulake has been quoted in the press in publications such as Bloomberg, Dow Jones, Reuters, Financial Times, the Chicago Tribune, Crain's Chicago Business, Futures Magazine and Advanced Trading. He has appeared on FOX Business Live and has spoken at numerous industry events involving topics such as high frequency trading, enterprise risk management, market data, and algorithmic trading.

Prior to joining Aite Group, Mr. Zubulake was the connectivity manager for the futures department at Citigroup Global Markets. Prior to that, he supervised trading at the Broketec Futures Exchange. Mr. Zubulake has also held trading and institutional sales positions in the futures and options space at REFCO Inc., Cresvale International LLC, and Finacor Vendome Inc.

Mr. Zubulake received his B.A. in Economics from the University of Maryland. He holds Series 3, Series 7, and Series 63 licenses.

SANG LEE

Sang Lee is a co-founder of Aite Group, LLC and currently serves as the managing partner. Mr. Lee's expertise lies in the securities and investments vertical and has advised many global financial institutions, software/hardware vendors, and professional services firms in sell-side and buy-side electronic trading technology and market structure.

Mr. Lee has been quoted extensively in the media, including the *Wall Street Journal, New York Times*, the *Washington Post, Financial Times, BusinessWeek, Newsday, CBS MarketWatch*, and *Investor's Business Daily*. He has also been quoted in, and written articles for, various trade publications, including *Pensions and Investments, Institutional Investor, Crain's New York Business, Wall Street & Technology, Euromoney, Trading Technology Week, Securities Industry News, Financial News, HedgeWorld, American Banker, Bank Technology News*, and *The Bond Buyer*.

Prior to joining Aite Group, Mr. Lee was a founding member of Celent Communications and served as the Manager of the Securities & Investments Group as well as the Operations Group. At Celent, Mr. Lee played a pivotal role in creating and growing one of the leading securities and investments practices in the financial services research industry.

Prior to Celent, Mr. Lee served as a business strategist for ZEFER, an industry-leading Internet professional services firm in Boston. At ZEFER, Mr. Lee formulated Internet business strategies for Fortune 1000 clients.

Index